Getting the Very Best From Your Scroll Saw

GETTING THE VERY BEST FROM YOUR SCROLL SAW

DON GEARY

POPULAR WOODWORKING BOOKS

CINCINNATI, OHIO

Read This Important Safety Notice

To prevent accidents, keep safety in mind while you work. Use the safety guards installed on power equipment; they are for your protection. When working on power equipment, keep fingers away from saw blades, wear safety goggles to prevent injuries from flying wood chips and sawdust, wear ear protection to protect your hearing, and consider installing a dust vacuum to reduce the amount of airborne sawdust in your woodshop. Don't wear loose clothing, such as neckties or shirts with loose sleeves, or jewelry, such as rings, necklaces or bracelets, when working on power equipment, and tie back long hair to prevent it from getting caught in your equipment. People who are sensitive to certain chemicals should check the chemical content of any product before using it. The author and editors who compiled this book have tried to make all the contents as accurate and correct as possible. Plans, illustrations, photographs and text have been carefully checked. All instructions, plans and projects should be carefully read, studied and understood before beginning construction. Due to the variability of local conditions, construction materials, skill levels, etc., neither the author nor Popular Woodworking Books assumes any responsibility for any accidents, injuries, damages or other losses incurred resulting from the material presented in this book.

Other fine Popular Woodworking Books are available from your local bookstore or direct from the publisher.

02 01 00 99 98   8 7 6 5 4

Library of Congress Cataloging-in-Publication Data

Geary, Don.
  Getting the very best from your scroll saw / by Don Geary.—
1st ed.
      p.   cm.
  Includes index.
  ISBN 1-55870-392-6 (alk. paper)
  1. Jig saws. I. Title.
TT186.G42 195
745.51—dc20   95-23672
                                                    CIP

Edited by Adam Blake
Content Editing by Thomas G. Begnal
Production Editing by Bruce E. Stoker
Cover and Interior Design by Brian Roeth
Computer Illustrations by Bob Shreve
Illustrations by Byron Williams

About the Author

Don Geary has been writing books and magazine articles for twenty years and specializes in home improvement, woodworking, tool working and related topics. He has been a member of the National Association of Home and Workshop Writers since 1976. Don also writes about the great outdoors and has been a member of the Outdoor Writer's Association since 1978.

Don lives with his wife and two sons in Salt Lake City, Utah, where home and office are one and the same. Don's future writing plans call for more how-to books on home improvement and outdoor topics.

Other Books by Don Geary

How to Design & Build Home Workshops
Woodworking Projects for the Great Outdoors
How to Sharpen Every Blade in Your Woodshop
The Welder's Bible

TABLE OF CONTENTS

INTRODUCTION

The scroll saw is one of the most popular woodworking tools in existence. Almost anyone from 10 to 100 years old who can learn how to make a variety of cuts can make truly professional-looking projects in a relatively short time. There is no gender barrier when it comes to scroll saws either—one manufacturer estimates that at least 30 percent of all sales are to women. Many scroll saw users have turned a hobby into a small business selling projects made in their spare time.

In this book you will learn the basics of scroll saw use. When you first begin, chances are your cuts will be a little rough until you master maneuvering a workpiece into the cutting blade. In the beginning stick with the simpler projects. After you become proficient, move on to the more advanced projects. In a short time you will be designing and making your own woodworking projects.

Every effort has been made in these pages to teach you how to safely use a scroll saw. While the scroll saw is probably the safest of all woodworking power tools, you can nevertheless injure yourself. To be safe, always use the safety equipment that came with your saw—specifically the clear plastic blade shield and the work hold-down foot. In addition, wear eye protection while working on your scroll saw. Finally, minimize distractions in your woodworking shop and concentrate on what you are trying to accomplish.

No book can be the work of one person; the book you hold in your hands is certainly no exception. I owe thanks to the folks at Sears Roebuck & Company, Dremel, Skil, Delta, Ryobi, Black & Decker, and DeWalt for tools supplied for testing and photographic purposes. I would also like to thank Adam Blake, my understanding editor at F&W Publications. My two sons—Bryan and Matthew—were helpful with many of the scroll saw projects even when we should have been fishing or hunting instead. Last, but certainly not least, I would like to thank my wife, Susan, for her support, encouragement and understanding during this writing project.

Don Geary   1995
Salt Lake City, Utah

CHAPTER ONE
Scroll Saw Anatomy

The scroll saw is one of the most useful sawing machines to have around the woodworking shop. With it one can cut intricate patterns not only in wood but also in plastic, nonferrous metals (aluminum, brass, copper), plaster and horn.

A scroll saw is one of the safest of all power cutting tools, and this, no doubt, has led to its overall popularity. Safe workshop procedures should always be practiced when using any power tool, but a scroll is probably the safest of all to use. In addition to male woodworkers, women have increasingly turned to the scroll saw for hobbies and crafts.

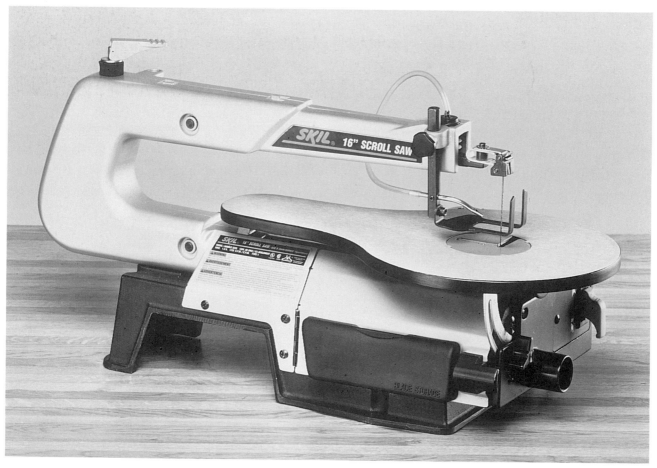

A scroll saw is a versatile woodworking power tool.

Anyone can quickly learn how to use a scroll saw.

One manufacturer estimates that roughly 30 percent of all sales are to women. Children as young as 10 years old can learn how to use a scroll saw—obviously with adult supervision—and can start cutting out projects in a short period of time.

The widespread popularity of the scroll saw is due in part to the low initial cost of entry-level units—currently under $125. Scroll saws in this group have a wide range of uses and are virtually ready to use right out of the box. While saw blades are consumable—they wear out and break frequently—their low cost (about fifty cents each) makes them one of the least expensive woodworking tools in your workshop.

The scroll saw is often compared to a band saw. While these two tools are similar, they are very different when it comes to the type of work that each can do.

As a rule, a band saw is used for cutting thicker material (over 2″-thick) and can accomplish cutting very quickly.

In general, a scroll saw makes smoother cuts than a band saw. In fact, a good scroll saw cut may not require any sanding. That can be a big advantage if your project has lots of edges that are difficult to sand.

Band saws cut with a continuous forward-cutting action and require much greater care and operator attention. This generally means that a band saw is potentially more dangerous than a scroll saw, which cuts with a reciprocating action.

Scroll saws, because they utilize a straight, nar-

A band saw is often compared to a scroll saw, but they are different.

row blade, can be used to cut sharper curves with much greater detail than can possibly be cut on a band saw. In addition, scroll saws can be used for making cuts inside the workpiece—the inside of the letter *P* or *O*, for example—because the scroll saw blade can be threaded through a hole drilled in the workpiece. Because a band-saw blade is a continuous loop, inside cuts are impossible.

Band saws require a number of adjustments to make them run properly. A scroll saw, on the other hand, is relatively free from adjustments and is therefore much easier to set up and use.

Basic Criteria

Scroll saws are described according to four criteria: cutting capacity, cutting speed, stroke length and throat capacity.

Cutting Capacity

Cutting capacity is simply the thickest material that can be cut with the unit. Most scroll saws will easily cut material up to 2″ thick; some of the larger models can cut material up to about 2¾″ thick.

Cutting Speed

The cutting speed of a scroll saw is commonly described in strokes per minute (spm). Variable-speed scroll saws which have a knob or dial that adjusts the blade speed for the work in progress are the most useful. When shopping for a scroll saw, you will be more satisfied with a unit that has variable speeds than with a unit that has a single speed.

Stroke Length

Stroke length is the distance the blade travels from top to bottom of its stroke. Small units generally have short stroke lengths, while larger units have longer stroke lengths. As a rule, the longer the stroke length, the cooler the blade will remain. Stroke lengths range from ⅝″ to 1¼″. Longer stroke lengths are generally more efficient, as they pull sawdust out of the cut more effectively.

Throat Capacity

Throat capacity—probably the most commonly used scroll saw classification—indicates the distance between the saw blade and the rear of the machine. A 14″-throat scroll saw can, for example, cut to the center of a piece of material that measures 28″ wide.

Types of Scroll Saws

The explosion of interest in scroll saws has not gone unnoticed by the manufacturers. You need only look at a tool catalog to see the wide choice of machines that are now available. At last count there were almost three dozen models.

Rigid-Arm Scroll Saws

As the name suggests, rigid-arm scroll saws have fixed arms. A system of coiled springs and pistons moves the blade up and down between the arms. However, the push-pull action acts to flex and fatigue the blades, and they seem to break all too quickly.

Rigid-arm scroll saws have been around for years, and a few manufacturers still make them. But, for the most part, they are being replaced by the new constant-tension scroll saws.

Constant-Tension Scroll Saws

The most popular scroll saw design currently on the market is commonly referred to as the constant-tension scroll saw. The saw is engineered so that the blade is stretched between the arms of the saw, keeping the blade in tension at all times, hence its name. Generally speaking, there are two types of constant-tension scroll saws: C-Arm and Parallel-Arm.

C-Arm Scroll Saws: C-Arm scroll saws have a single pivot point, which means that the blade tilts back ever so slightly on each upstroke. The result is a generally less precise cutting action, especially when cutting sharp curves in stock thicker than ¾″.

Parallel-Arm Scroll Saws: These saws have two pivot points, resulting in a blade sawing action that is always perfectly vertical. As a result, the cuts will always be vertical when the saw table is set perpendicular to the blade.

It is probably safe to say that parallel-arm scroll saws are the most popular of all the scroll saws on the market today. Parallel-arm saws, because of their popularity, are really the basis for this book.

Parallel-Arm Scroll Saw Features

Parallel-arm scroll saws vary in price depending on the variety of features that are on the unit. While operation is similar between all types of parallel-arm scroll saws, special features and sizes make one unit more versatile than another. As a rule, a more expensive parallel-arm scroll saw will have a number of features that are not available on lesser priced units. Let's take a look at the features currently available on parallel-arm scroll saws.

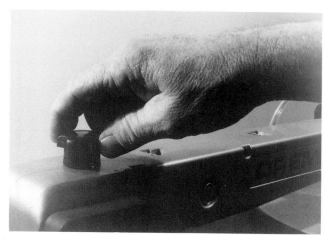

Some scroll saws have an adjusting knob on the rear of the upper arm.

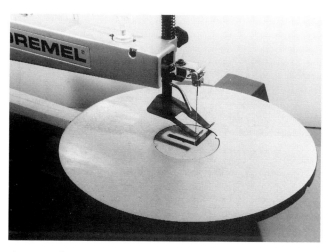

A cast aluminum or cast iron scroll saw table will help to reduce vibration while the saw is running.

A tilt table is necessary for making bevel cuts on a scroll saw.

Arms

The arms are probably the most obvious characteristic of all parallel-arm scroll saws. These arms are commonly made from cast aluminum or cast iron. A blade-tension control knob is usually located at the rear end of the arm, while the front end will have a visible blade clamp (for the top end of a saw blade). On smaller units the arms may be covered by some type of housing—a feature that adds to safe operation of the saw; on larger units the top arm is often exposed.

Base

The base of all parallel-arm scroll saws supports the upper structure and conceals the lower arm, electrical wiring and other components. Bases are made from sheet steel, cast aluminum or cast iron. Some base units are made to be bolted directly to a workbench, while others are bolted to a special workstand. As a rule, a cast base will greatly reduce vibration and be easier to work on than a unit that has a lightweight base.

Table

The table or baseplate on a parallel-arm scroll saw is quite important, as it supports the work during cutting. Scroll saw tables are commonly made from cast aluminum or cast iron. When shopping for a parallel-arm scroll saw, avoid inexpensive units that have a stamped steel table; this type is noisy and not as dependable as the cast types. A handy feature of many parallel-arm scroll saws on the market is a pivoting table that permits bevel cuts.

The blade slot on a parallel-arm scroll saw will vary among manufacturers. Some simply have a circular hole in which the scroll saw blade operates, while others have a slot that runs all the way to the front of the table. A small plastic or metal disk should fit around the blade to support the work as it is being cut.

Motors

The electric motor of any parallel-arm scroll saw produces the power to run the unit. Electric motors are rated by horsepower (hp) and can range from $\frac{1}{10}$ hp in the small units to $\frac{1}{4}$ hp in large, freestanding parallel-arm scroll saws.

Drives

An electric motor is used to drive the lower arm in parallel-arm scroll saws. This power can be transferred to the arm in any of four different ways. Direct drive (single speed of about 1,725 spm) is one method. A second method utilizes a two-speed motor controlled by a selector switch; the low speed is usually around 900 spm, and the high speed is usually around 1,725 spm.

A belt-drive system is the third means of powering a parallel-arm scroll saw. The most common belt drive involves a stepped pulley that provides a range of one, two, three or four fixed speeds. To change from one speed to another, the belt must be repositioned on the stepped pulley. This can be a time-consuming process.

Speed Control

By far the most convenient means of powering a parallel-arm scroll saw is by a variable-speed control switch or dial. This popular power system offers quick changes in reciprocating speed. Some units have an LCD screen that indicates the spm speed; this is a worthwhile feature.

Air Blower

An air-blowing system is another common feature on many parallel-arm scroll saws. An air blower is simply an air-pumping bellows that forces air down a hose to a small nozzle located around the cutting blade. In theory, the air blower provides a constant

This LCD screen indicates exact strokes per minute.

Sawdust blowers are designed to blow sawdust away from the cut line.

supply of air through a hose to a nozzle to blow sawdust away from the blade, enabling the user to clearly see the cut line. In practice, all air blowers seem a bit inadequate and require tinkering with to get near-acceptable performance. In the next chapter you will learn how to make an inexpensive sawdust blower that is much more effective.

Hold-Down

All parallel-arm scroll saws have a hold-down mechanism that helps keep the material flat on the table while being cut. Without such a device, the material would vibrate and move up and down during cutting. A hold-down also helps define the cut area and acts as a safety feature that helps to prevent you from coming in contact with the moving blade.

Blade Guard

A blade guard is another safety feature found on all parallel-arm scroll saws. Commonly made of clear plastic, a blade guard shields the area around the blade and allows you to work.

As a rule, never operate a parallel-arm scroll

A work hold-down foot will help you to control the workpiece.

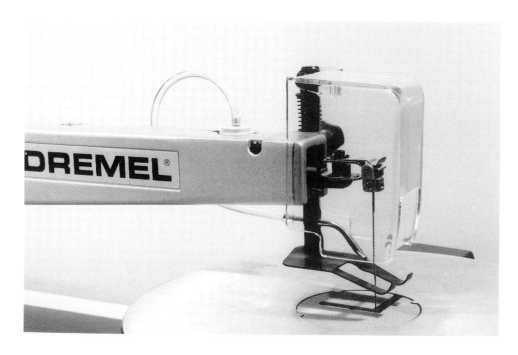

A blade guard is a safety feature that will prevent mishap.

saw without both the hold-down mechanism and blade guard in place. Having said this, you should know that there will be some instances where these safety devices will get in the way and make cutting more difficult. I personally recommend that these safety features always be used. You, on the other hand, may be inclined to remove these safety features once you become proficient with working on a scroll saw. Know in advance that you greatly increase the chances of mishap by removing these safety devices.

Blade Tensioning

Blade-tension adjustment devices are commonly located on the rear end of the top arm on parallel-arm scroll saws; newer models have an adjustment knob, the most common means of adjusting the tension on a scroll saw blade, located at the front of the arm. The knob is turned in one direction to increase the tension and in the opposite direction to decrease the tension.

A much quicker means of adjusting blade tension involves the use of a lever. As you can imagine, this method is very fast. Unfortunately, this type of blade-tension adjustment lever is not widely used on scroll saws.

Blade Attachment

The way a scroll saw blade is held between the arms of a parallel-arm scroll saw—most commonly by special blade holders—is very important. The holders have a dual purpose: to securely hold the blade during the cutting operation and at the same time to pivot or rock during operation. It is safe to say that one of the most important design features of any scroll saw is how the blade holders do their job; many of the problems associated with scroll saws can be directly traced to poorly designed or improperly operating blade holders. There are design differences among manufacturers, and consequently some holders are easier to work with than others. To help you understand how blade holders work, let's look at the two most popular means of holding a scroll saw blade in place.

Easily, the simplest blade holder system secures a pin-end scroll saw blade in a grooved bracket attached to the leading edge of both arms on a parallel-arm scroll saw. This type of blade holder is very easy to use: Simply loosen the tension-adjustment knob, remove the dull blade, install a new blade with teeth pointing downward, and readjust the tension. In use, the pin (which passes through both ends of the blade) rides and rocks in the grooved slot. This type of blade holder is popular

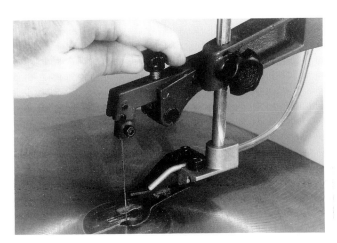

Blade tensioning knob located at the front end of the upper arm.

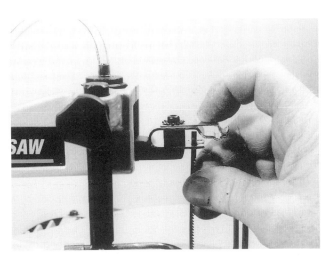

Pin-end scroll saw blade holder bracket.

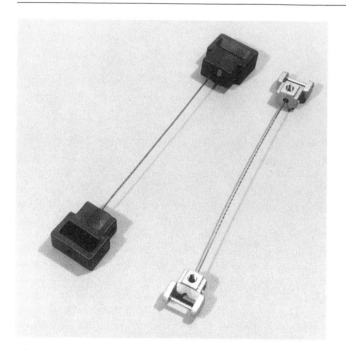

Blade clamps vary between manufacturers, but all work in a similar manner.

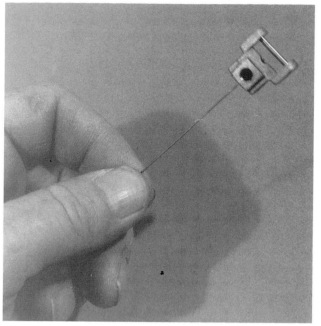

Blade clamp holders are necessary for installing a new blade in the clamps.

on many types of scroll saws and is really ideal for pin-end scroll saw blades.

Unfortunately, pin-end scroll saw blades are much wider than plain-end scroll saw blades, and this can present a problem when cutting intricate patterns. For really detailed cutting your best choice will be a plain-end scroll saw blade, and these require special clamps to hold the blade between the arms on a parallel-arm scroll saw. At this time all such clamps hold a blade by means of a small set screw, which must be tightened using an Allen wrench. These clamps are called parallel flat-jaw blade clamps, and while they differ from manufacturer to manufacturer, they all work pretty much the same.

Many parallel-arm scroll saws have special indents on the top of the machine which hold the two clamps while you position and fasten the blade in place. Some manufacturers offer a special T-shaped Allen wrench while others simply offer a conventional Allen wrench.

Scroll Saw Blades

Saw blades are the business end of any scroll saw, and you will be amazed at the number of different types, styles and sizes available. Scroll saw blades are also one of the least expensive woodworking tools you can purchase—currently prices range from about fifty cents to a dollar each, with lower prices commonly offered for buying in quantity.

In truth there is not one single scroll saw blade that can be used for all types of cutting. Instead, there are many different types of scroll saw blades designed for rather specific cutting tasks. Choosing the right type of blade for the cutting task at hand is not particularly difficult—all saws come with recommendations as to the best blade choice for a specific cutting operation. You will also find a suggested blade usage chart on page 14. As a general guideline, the right blade will depend on your saw type, the material type and thickness you are cutting, the complexity of the cuts you are making, the cutting speed of your saw, and the cut-edge finish

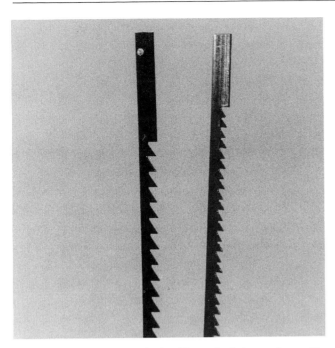

Pin-end scroll saw blade (l) and plain-end scroll saw blade (r).

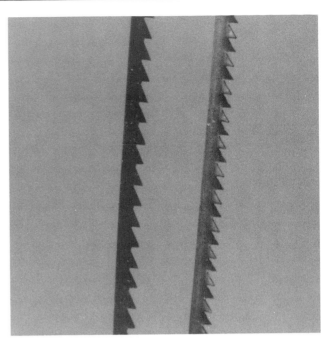

10 teeth-per-inch blade (l) and 20 teeth-per-inch blade (r).

you would like (smooth or general purpose, for example).

All scroll saw blades fall into two rather broad categories: pin-end and plain-end blades. As a rule, plain-end scroll saw blades come in a greater variety of sizes and tooth patterns, which makes them popular for intricate cutting tasks. Pin-end scroll saw blades, on the other hand, are much easier to use and are therefore popular for general cutting tasks.

Pin-End Scroll Saw Blades

Pin-end scroll saw blades are commonly described in teeth-per-inch; this is an indication of how smoothly they will cut most wooden materials. As a rule, and this holds true for all types of saw blades, the greater number of teeth-per-inch, the smoother the finished cut edges will be. A scroll saw blade with 20 teeth-per-inch, for example, will produce a cut that is considered a finish cut—little or no sanding will be required before finishing. A scroll saw with 10 teeth-per-inch is more suitable

There are many different types of scroll saw blades for a variety of scroll sawing tasks.

for fast, rough cutting—the cut edges will require sanding to remove saw marks. Pin-end scroll saw blades are good for general cutting and some finishing in the shop.

Plain-End Scroll Saw Blades

Plain-end scroll saw blades are available in a much wider range of types than pin-end scroll saw blades and are therefore more popular for serious scroll saw work. Generally speaking there are three basic types of plain-end scroll saw blades: scroll blades, fret blades and spiral blades.

Scroll Blades. Scroll blades are similar to the types offered in pin-end scroll saw blades. They are used primarily for coarse, general purpose cutting. They are better suited for cutting thicker materials and really hard wood, such as maple, oak and the harder exotic woods.

Fret Blades. Fret blades are popular for serious

scroll work. They are much thinner than conventional scroll saw blades and can therefore be used for cutting fine or intricate designs. All fret saw blades have a skip-tooth design—every other tooth is missing—which helps to remove sawdust from the cut more quickly and results in a cooler blade than a regular tooth design. A cooler cutting blade will stay sharp and last longer than other types.

Reverse-Tooth Blades. One variation to the basic fret blade is called the reverse-tooth blade. This blade has the bottom inch or so of the teeth facing upward, while the remainder of the teeth point downward in the conventional manner. Different patterns are available, such as blades having six, seven or nine bottom teeth facing upward. This tooth configuration is ideal for sawing plywood— the problem of the bottom cut splintering is eliminated by this design.

In addition to regular skip-tooth fret blades, double-tooth-skip scroll saw blades are also available. These are a relatively new design and a good

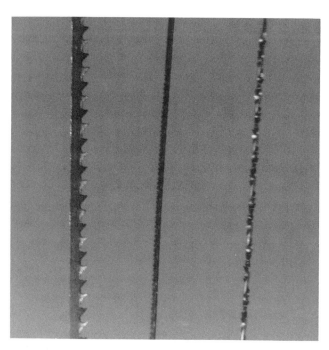

Three basic types of plain-end scroll saw blades: (l to r) scroll, fret and spiral.

Skip-tooth scroll saw blade design.

choice for beginners who want to learn the basics of scroll saw work.

Spiral Blades. Spiral scroll saw blades are the last type of blade of interest to woodworkers. Spiral blades are simply conventional scroll saw blades that have been machine twisted so their teeth point outward in all directions. As you can imagine, spiral blades enable you to make very sharp turns in the workpiece. Spiral scroll saw blades are available in fine- and medium-tooth patterns and are therefore suitable for a variety of finish cutting applications. Spiral scroll saw blades can be difficult to work with for the beginner as they tend to make a wider cutting path (kerf) than conventional blades and also require the operator to control the movement of the workpiece with greater care—spiral blades tend to follow the grain of the workpiece. Nevertheless, once you become proficient at scroll sawing, you will find spiral blades handy for making a variety of intricate cuts in all types of material—light metals, bone, horn and plaster.

Jewelers' Blades. The last type of scroll saw blade that you may come in contact with is the jewelers' blade. These are made of hardened, tempered steel and are used for cutting thin (sheet) nonferrous

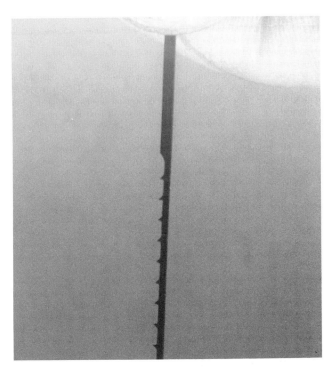

Reverse-tooth scroll saw blade design.

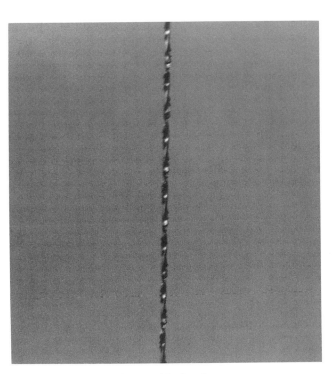

Spiral-tooth scroll saw blade design.

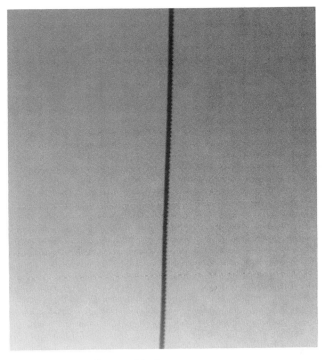

Jewelers' scroll saw blade.

A Guide to Scroll Saw Blades

Materials	Size	Plain End 2/0 28 TPI	2 20 TPI	5 12.5 TPI	7 11.5 TPI	12 9.5 TPI	Metal Piercing 1 48 TPI	5 36 TPI	7 30 TPI	Pin end 7 15 TPI	7 10 TPI	2/0 18.5 TPI	Spiral 0 46 TPI	2 41 TPI	Speed
SOFTWOODS															
Basswood	1/4"			●								●			1200-2000
	1/2"			●								●			1500-2000
	3/4"				●							●			1700-2000
	1 1/8"					●						●			2000
	2"					●						●			2000
Soft pine or Redwood	1/4"			●								●			1400-2000
	1/2"			●								●			1600-2000
	3/4"				●							●			1800-2000
	1 1/8"					●						●			2000
	2"					●						●			2000
Yellow pine	1/4"			●								●			1400-2000
	1/2"				●							●			1600-2000
	3/4"				●							●			1800-2000
	1 1/8"					●						●			2000
	2"					●						●			2000
HARDWOODS															
Oak (white or red) Walnut, Cherry	1/4"			●								●			140-2000
	1/2"				●							●			1600-2000
	3/4"					●						●			1600-2000
	1 1/8"					●						●			1800-2000
	2"					●						●			2000
PLYWOOD															
Plywood veneer	1/32	●										●			300-600
Plywood or Particle board	1/4"			●								●			800-1800
	1/2"				●							●			1200-1800
	3/4"					●						●			1600-2000
Baltic birch Plywood	1/8"		●	●											800-1400
	1/4"			●								●			1200-1800
	1/2"				●							●			1400-2000
	3/4"					●						●			1600-2000
8-1/8 pieces stacked	1"					●						●			2000
PLASTICS															
ABS plastic sheet	1/4"											●			800-1000
ABS water pipe	2"					●						●			900-1100
Plexiglass	1/4"											●			300-700
	1/2"					●						●			400-500
METALS															
Copper sheet	1/8"						●	●							500-700
	1/4"								●						400-600
Copper pipe	3/4"								●						500-700
Yellow brass	3/32"							●	●						1100-1400
	1/4"								●						900-1200
Aluminum	1/8"							●	●						700
	1/4"								●						600
Soft steel & galvanized sheet	16g.							●							600-800
Low carbon plate or cast metal	1/4"								●						350-550
OTHER															
Masonite—plain or tempered	1/4"			●								●			1600-2000
Sheet rock, wallboard, ceiling tile, particle board	3/4"				●	●				●					1600-2000

metals, such as copper, brass and aluminum. They can also be used for cutting thin steel. As a rule, jewelers' scroll saw blades are not suitable for cutting wood, as the teeth are too close together and tend to clog. These blades are similar to hacksaw blades when compared to a conventional crosscut saw blade—a hack saw blade is not suitable for cutting wood either, but it is the blade of choice when cutting metal.

Choosing the Right Scroll Saw Blade

A number of important factors will influence your choice of a scroll saw blade for a given project. Know in advance that no single scroll saw blade can be considered all purpose or should be used for all cutting operations. The major factors that will influence your choice of a scroll saw blade include the thickness and type of material being cut, the cutting and feed speeds, and the intricacy of the pattern being cut.

As a general guideline, thin materials can be cut easily with a fine (greater number of teeth-per-inch) blade, but as the material thickness increases, the number of teeth-per-inch must decrease. In short, thick material requires cutting with a scroll saw blade with fewer teeth-per-inch than thinner material.

The same is true for the type of material being cut. Hardwoods—oak, maple, cherry, walnut and birch, for example—are more easily cut with coarser blades. Softwoods—pine, basswood, balsa and veneers—can all be cut with fine scroll saw blades. The chart on page 14 can be used as a further guide to scroll saw blades.

Most of the scroll saw blades you will come in contact with are stamped by a machine, which results in a blade that is rougher on one side—most

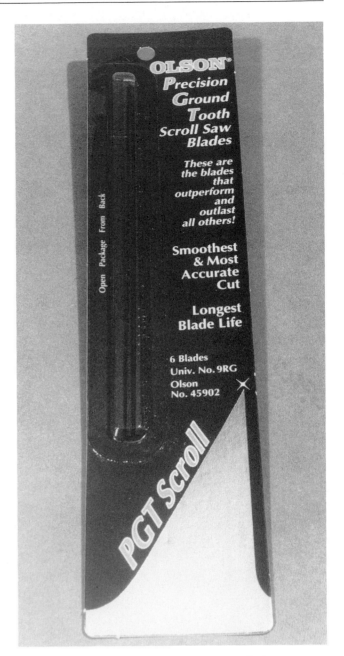

Olson Precision Ground scroll saw blades are among the finest available.

commonly the right side. This means that the blade will pull to one side. Some blade manufacturers, such as Olson, offer precision-ground scroll saw blades. Although precision-ground blades are more expensive, they will cut much cleaner patterns than machine-stamped blades.

CHAPTER TWO

Scroll Saw Techniques From the Pros

This chapter contains a wealth of information I and many other woodworkers have gleaned over the years. It is divided into useful sections that cover material selection, fine tuning scroll saws, and how to make a useful sawdust-blower system. You will learn how to make patterns from various materials and how to transfer patterns to the workpiece. You will also gain insight into how to design and make your own patterns from a universe of choices.

Finally, information is also offered on how to make several types of cuts that will save time and generally make scroll sawing more interesting.

Materials

A scroll saw can be used to cut a wide range of materials in addition to the obvious woods, plywood

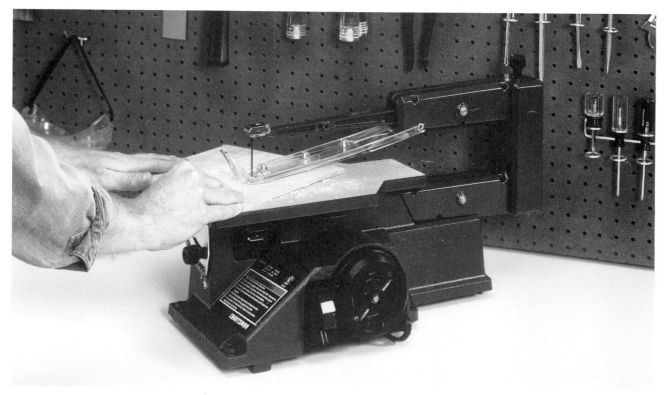

Any scroll saw can easily cut thin plywood.

and veneers commonly associated with woodworking projects. It can easily cut most types of plastic, sheet metals (both ferrous and nonferrous), bone, horn and even glass. Special blades are usually required for harder materials. Since the majority of the projects in this book—and those that you are likely to make—will be constructed from wood, this section will cover the types available.

Hardwood and Softwood

A scroll saw can be used for cutting any type of hardwood or softwood. A larger scroll saw (larger throat) will be required for cutting thicker pieces, but a small, hobbyist scroll saw can be used for cutting all types of thinner (less than 1″ thick) hardwoods or softwoods, as well as plywood. Some general comments about woods should prove helpful when selecting a wood for a given project.

One of the most important points to consider about solid wood is the density. Uniformity is the key and will determine how easy or hard the stock will be to work. Trying to saw through a piece of stock that has changes in density is annoying—soft areas will cut quickly, but when the blade comes in contact with a much denser area, it will almost come to a stop. Trying to follow your pattern cut line is also difficult when the density of the wood changes. Soft areas will grab the blade; hard areas will deflect the blade so it cuts off the line. All this adds up to difficult sawing and ragged edges.

As a rule, hardwoods such as oak, soft maple, basswood, walnut and poplar all scroll saw quite nicely. Softwoods such as pine, cedar, redwood and fir are popular for scroll saw projects but can often be difficult to work with because they lack uniform density. Dimensional lumber—construction lumber such as 2×4, 2×6, 2×8 and 2×10—is popular for scroll saw projects simply because of availability. When selecting lumber for projects, look for pieces that have more uniform colors in the grain—dark

A scroll saw can be used to cut a wide range of materials.

growth rings will be much harder than sapwood and are much harder to saw.

You will find flat-sawn material—both hardwood and softwood—saws more smoothly than any other type of solid lumber. When choosing material for a project, look for boards that have an end grain runs parallel to the cutting surface. If at all possible, avoid quartersawn material (grain runs vertical when viewed from the end of the board) as the grain will tend to stall the blade and make accurately following a pattern difficult.

When you are working on a tight woodworking budget, look carefully at no. 3 grade pine instead of typically clearer no. 2 grade pine. Often you can trace your pattern in such a way as to avoid knots and other imperfections in the lesser grade pine. If the project will be painted, you should consider using no. 3 grade pine because the lower initial cost can add up to significant savings over time.

Plywood

Plywood is very popular and practical for many scroll saw projects. This is particularly true when

When using dimensional lumber, choose pieces that do not have a lot of grain contrast.

Flatsawn lumber (l), where grain runs parallel to cutting surface, is a better choice for scroll saw projects than quartersawn lumber (r), where grain runs perpendicular to the cutting surface.

using thin material that is prone to breakage when the grain runs across a narrow part of the material—a bird's beak, for example. In some cases it is possible to align the grain to avoid this problem, but at other times plywood is the only practical answer to the problem.

Easily, the most common type of plywood is construction grade, and as a rule this is probably the poorest choice for most scroll saw projects. Construction grade plywood (commonly labeled CDX) often has voids in interior layers and knots and plugs on the surfaces. There are much better, although more expensive, grades of plywood for

scroll saw projects. Let's take a closer look at plywood so you will be aware of the many choices currently available.

All plywood can be lumped into two very broad categories: exterior and interior grades. In addition, there are a number of grade designations within these two groups.

Exterior grade plywood is made with a special waterproof glue. Such a panel can be exposed to the weather for an indefinite period of time without any ply delamination. There are many grades within the exterior classification; as a rule, if your scroll saw project is intended for outdoor use—decoys or

For economy, trace your pattern carefully to avoid knots on #3 grade lumber.

Plugs and internal voids are common on construction grade plywood.

whirligigs, for example—you should only use exterior grade plywood.

Interior grade plywood is made with a glue that could theoretically be affected by moisture; all interior grade plywood is made with a highly moisture resistant (but not waterproof) adhesive. In practice, many interior types of plywood and all exterior types of plywood are manufactured with a special exterior glue.

Another basic difference between exterior and interior grades of plywood is that the interior grades are generally considered to be appearance grades. They are designed to be used inside a home where they will be more visible than exterior uses—cabinets, for example.

There is also the designation engineered grade for both interior and exterior plywood. Basically, engineered grade means that the ultimate use of the plywood will be in some type of concealed installation. Examples of this type of installation include subfloor sheeting and roof or deck sheeting. As you can well imagine, there is quite a bit of difference between a sheet of plywood that will be used for a roof or deck and one that is used for an interior wall covering. Keep this difference in mind when shopping for plywood: If the project will be painted, almost any type of plywood can be used, but if the project is to be left in a natural state or finished

with a clear coating, then an appearance grade plywood should be used.

Generally, engineered grades of plywood will have a number of patches or plugs on both the face and back of the panel, and the panel will not have a smooth, sanded finish. Appearance grades of plywood are available with face and back panels in a wide range of hardwoods and softwoods.

In addition to the plywood and solid wood available at your local lumberyard, consider mail-order sources for these same materials. A number of mail-order companies (see Appendix) offer a good selection of lumber and plywood for scroll saw projects. In some cases these companies offer a selection of hardwoods, softwoods and plywoods found nowhere else. You may want to turn to these sources for special needs, even though the prices are not competitive.

Metal

When most woodworkers think of a scroll saw, they think only of cutting wood. In truth a scroll saw equipped with a special blade can be used to cut a wide range of materials, including metal, plastic, horn and ivory.

Aluminum and brass are the easiest and best metals to cut on a scroll saw; don't try to cut ferrous metals (iron and steel). The keys to success when cutting metal include using a special jewelers' (metal-piercing) blade and a slow saw speed. Jewelers' scroll saw blades are much harder than conventional wood-cutting blades and have more teeth-per-inch.

Metal-piercing blades are not as forgiving as woodworking blades and therefore break often. When cutting wood, a conventional blade can handle some side pressure, but when cutting metal, forcing the work sideways will cause the metal-cutting blade to heat up quickly and break. Always feed the work straight into the metal-cutting blade, and this problem will be minimized. This is especially important when making turn cuts in metal—strive to keep the force on the front of the blade at all times.

Metal-cutting blades also require some type of lubrication during use. Good choices include beeswax, silicone spray, kitchen shortening and sewing machine oil. Reapply lubricant often to keep the blade cool and cutting smoothly.

When cutting thin sheet metal, sandwich it between two pieces of ⅛"- to ½"-thick scrap lumber. Fasten the pieces together with tape, double-stick tape or a suitable adhesive. Transfer your pattern to the top layer and cut out carefully.

When cutting thicker metal, attach your pattern directly to the face of the piece with rubber cement.

Cover the bottom of the piece with masking tape or clear packing tape to prevent scratching. Do not try to cut a small piece of metal—it will be difficult to maneuver into the scroll saw blade. If the finished project is small, start with a large piece, cut the detail, then make the final cuts. Use plenty of lubricant when cutting thick metal to keep the blade cool and to help it cut more efficiently.

Shopping for metal for scroll saw projects can be difficult. Aluminum is generally available at home improvement centers, hobby and model shops, and from retail metal dealers (look in the Yellow Pages under Fabricators, Metal). As a rule, soft aluminum up to about ⅛"-thick will cut well on almost any scroll saw. Thicker aluminum is more difficult to cut and is a slow process at best. Avoid alloyed

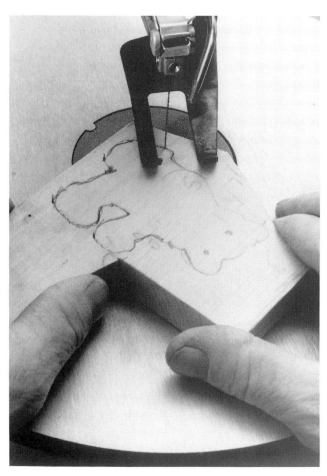

Appearance grade plywood is a good choice for most scroll saw projects.

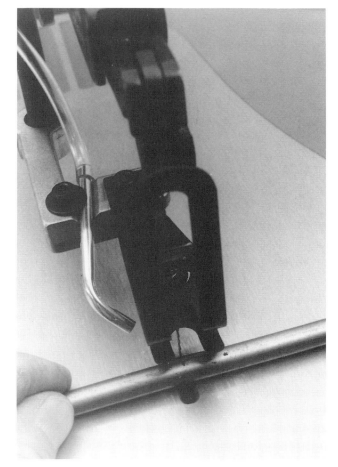

Aluminum and brass up to ¼" thick can be cut on most saws equipped with a jewelers' blade.

aluminum as it tends to be harder and more difficult to cut.

Brass suitable for scroll sawing can be very difficult to find. As with aluminum, try hobby and craft shops and also look in the Yellow Pages under Brass and Copper (brass is an alloy of copper). Thinner brass (1/8″) cuts well, but brass thicker than 1/4″ inch will test the limits of any scroll saw.

Metal Finishing. Metal projects can be finished in the home workshop in a number of ways, including polish, clear or satin finish, or brush-finish. For all finishing methods, after the project has been cut and drilled (if required) to your satisfaction, file or sand off burrs or rough edges.

Polishing produces a good finish for many metal

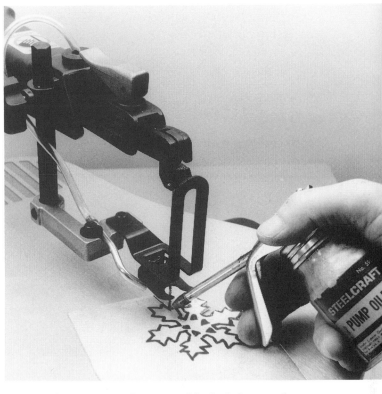

Always keep a metal-cutting blade lubricated during use.

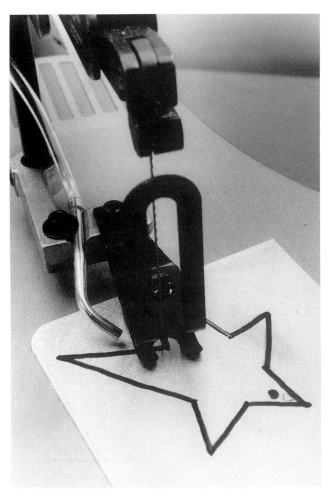

Always feed metal straight into a scroll saw blade.

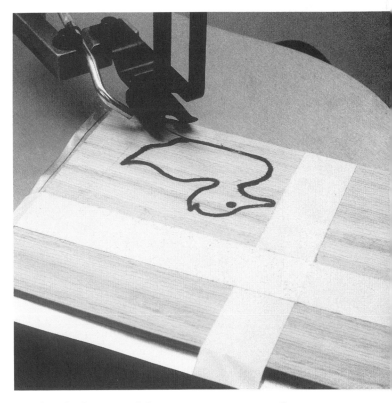

Sandwich thin metal between two pieces of scrap lumber before cutting.

File edges of a metal project after cutting and before finishing.

Metal can be polished on a Dremel vertical sander equipped with a buffing belt.

projects and is best accomplished on a buffing wheel or by hand polishing. Buffing wheels can be mounted on a bench grinder or electric drill; Dremel offers buffing attachments for its vertical belt sander. To polish metal, begin by charging the buffing wheel with polishing compound (commonly available in stick form). Brass and aluminum polish nicely with tripoli (brown) polishing compound. Simply press the compound stick against the spinning wheel, then hold the metal against the wheel to polish. You don't need to press too hard; let the wheel and polishing compound do the work for you. Small pieces can be difficult to polish. Wear gloves and eye protection to prevent injury when polishing metal.

A clear or satin finish can be achieved by polishing the project with automotive body rubbing compound. Follow the directions on the can and apply the compound by hand using a soft, clean cloth. You may also want to try any of the special metal polishes available at your local supermarket. There are polishing compounds for silver, brass, aluminum and gold.

To achieve a brushed finish, rub the surface with steel wool or fine (at least 600) grit emery cloth.

To achieve a brushed finish on metal projects, sand the surface with 600- to 1200-grit emery cloth. Steel wool can also be used. Keep in mind that the coarser the grit (lower the number) the rougher the finished surface. The motion you use to sand will result in a pattern: A circular motion will give the finish a swirl effect. If you want fine lines as a finish, sand in one direction only. Whichever motion you use, be consistent or some areas will have a more pronounced texture than others.

As a final finish to all metal projects, spray with a clear coating such as Krylon. This finish is available in flat, semigloss and high gloss. When applying, keep in mind the fact that metal does not absorb a finish the way wood does, so two or three light coats are much preferred over one heavy coat. Spray lightly from a distance of about 12 inches and allow each coat to dry before applying the next one.

Plastic

Scroll saws can be used to cut most types of plastic, although some types cut much more readily than

Metal projects can be polished with a liquid or paste polish.

Spray a clear coating on your metal project to protect the finish.

others. Plastics range in types from the softest (Styrofoam) to the harder types such as Plexiglas and countertop materials such as Formica and Corian. Some thermoplastics—those that can be shaped when warm—do not as a rule cut well on a scroll saw. Plastics tend to chip; to overcome this problem, place masking tape over the area to be cut and trace your pattern over the tape. The tape will minimize chipping.

Most plastics will cut better at a low speed. A thick, coarse (13 to 18 teeth-per-inch) blade will generally cut better than a finer (more teeth-per-inch) blade. Spiral blades and reversed blades are usually more effective at cutting plastics as well.

In all cases, make test cuts on a sample of plastic before actually starting a project to determine if the plastic you are considering for your project is, in fact, suitable.

Plexiglas up to ¼″ thick cuts well on a scroll saw. I have found a spiral blade works well for any type of detail cutting. For less involved cutting, try a scroll blade with 15 teeth-per-inch. Plexiglas also makes an ideal material for pattern templates—it is relatively easy to cut, you can see wood grain as you are tracing the pattern, and the template will last a lifetime.

Patterns

There are easily fifty different patterns contained in this book, and thousands of other patterns aimed specifically at the scroll sawyer are available from a variety of sources. Books of scroll saw patterns are plentiful and handy. Some mail-order companies sell full-size pattern sets for scroll saw projects. If you have a home (or office) computer, you probably also have a selection of clip art that can be adapted to scroll saw designs. In addition, the world is full of shapes and designs that can be adapted to scroll saw patterns. Some of the more obvious choices include wallpaper, gift wrapping, greeting cards, coloring books, stickers, decals and magazine photographs. Use your imagination and a copy machine to help you develop unique designs for your scroll saw projects.

Undoubtedly the easiest way to develop a pattern for scroll saw use is with a modern copier with enlarging and reducing capabilities that can be used to adapt patterns that are truly custom. When you first begin finding, tracing and cutting scroll saw projects, you may want to stick with stock patterns. As you become more familiar with how your saw works and how it cuts, however, you will probably want to let your creative forces take over and develop your own patterns. In many cases, you can use existing patterns as a basis for developing your own designs.

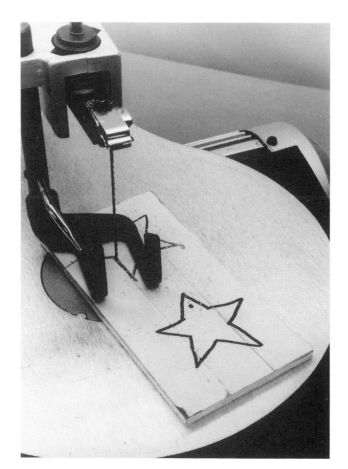

Use masking tape when cutting plastic to prevent chipping.

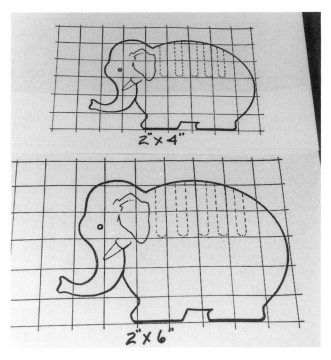

The world is full of scroll saw pattern possibilities.

A basic design enlarged and reduced on a copying machine.

Transferring Patterns

Once you have a pattern for a project, you must first transfer it to the material to be cut. There are several ways of doing this; to some extent the method you choose will depend on the design (simple or complex) and the material being sawed (wood, metal or plastic).

Probably the easiest way to transfer a pattern to the workpiece is with carbon paper. Simply lay the carbon paper over the desired area, place the pattern on top, and trace the outline of the pattern. It is important not to move the parts around until the entire design has been transferred. Use tape, thumbtacks, pushpins or staples to hold everything in place as you trace the pattern. Use a soft (#1) lead pencil with a rounded, not pointed, tip.

When tracing a pattern, use aids, such as a ruler, compass, circle templates and even coins, to help you get lines uniform. As a rule, freehand designs leave a bit to be desired, so it is always best to use tracing aids when you can.

Carbon paper is usually the first choice for trans-

Use carbon paper to transfer your design to the workpiece.

Mount patterns directly to the workpiece using a spray adhesive.

Plexiglas makes an ideal template material, as you can see grain clearly when laying out and tracing the design.

ferring a pattern to wood, but it can be a poor choice because the "carbon" can get messy. A better choice is graphite paper (available in artist supply stores), which does not smudge and can be erased. Additionally, graphite paper is available in light colors, which make patterns easy to see on dark-colored woods.

Another method of transferring a design to a workpiece is to apply the pattern itself to the work. The quickest and easiest way to do this is to use a spray adhesive such as Zenolyte Holdit! or 3M's Scotch Spray Mount Artist's Adhesive #6065. Rubber cement can also be used. In either case, apply or spray the adhesive to the back of the paper pattern—not the wood—wait a few seconds for the adhesive to become tacky, then apply the pattern to the workpiece. Smooth with your hand to remove any air bubbles, and you are ready for cutting. After the pattern has been cut out, simply peel off the pattern. Spray adhesive does not usually leave any residue; rubber cement does, but you can rub the residue off with your finger.

Templates are another way of transferring your pattern to the workpiece. It makes sense to use a template whenever you plan on making more than two or three pieces of the same project. Templates can be made from cardboard, poster board, thin plywood, sheet metal, Plexiglas or other suitable material. Plexiglas is one of the best materials because you can clearly see the grain through the template and can therefore position the template to take the best advantage of the grain. Ready-made templates are also available from craft and hobby shops.

To trace a pattern, position the template and then trace with a sharp pencil. For light-colored woods, use a dark pencil; for dark-colored woods, use a light pencil. You want contrast between the pattern lines and the workpiece which will help you to see the pattern lines when sawing.

Stack Cutting

Stack cutting is simply the process of cutting two or more pieces at the same time. This procedure not only saves time—it takes only slightly longer to cut several pieces than it does to cut one—but you can be certain that all pieces will be identical. One last bonus is that you only have to transfer the pattern to the top piece, and this can save time, especially when the pattern is intricate. If pilot holes are required, make them through the top piece after the stack has been completed.

In some cases—when sawing very thin veneer, for example—it will be necessary to sandwich the material prior to sawing to prevent feathering of the bottom edges. Sandwiching can also be used when cutting sheet metal and thin plastics.

There are several ways of sandwiching work-

Stack cutting saves time and ensures identical pieces.

Nail through waste areas to make stacks.

pieces together prior to sawing. One way is to simply nail, screw or staple the pieces together, but this method is only practical if there is a lot of waste material on the project through which you can drive nails or staples.

Another way of fastening workpieces together is to use double-stick tape. Double-stick carpet tape is generally available and works well to hold several pieces together while sawing.

Hot glue can also be used for holding pieces together when stack-sawing. Place a drop of hot glue in each of the corners of the bottom piece and quickly attach a second layer. Repeat the process for as many pieces as you want to stack together. This method works well when the corners are considered scrap material and you want to start sawing immediately.

If you have more time, consider using woodworking glue or adhesive. Once again, place a drop of glue at each corner, lay on another piece, and repeat the process until you have the required number of pieces in the stack. Next, clamp the bundle together overnight and begin sawing the next day.

Bevel Sawing

Most scroll sawing requires that the blade be at a perfect 90° angle to the table of the saw. When a project is cut in this manner, the cut piece can be pushed up or down in the waste material with ease. When the same cut is made with the table tilted, the cut piece can only be removed one way, as the top edge will be wider than the bottom edge of the cut. Bevel cutting can result in some interesting design possibilities—such as raised letters on a sign, veneer and solid-wood marquetry, inlay and intarsia, and even wooden bowl making—as you will see in later chapters.

While almost any project can be cut out with

Double-stick carpet tape is handy for making stacks.

Hot-melt glue can be used to make stacks quickly.

This shape is raised on one side, lowered on the other.

the table tilted, some designs do not lend themselves well to bevel cutting. Sharp details are difficult to impossible when bevel cutting, for example. Another point to consider is the thickness of the material. A piece of wood that is ¾" thick will require a saw that can handle 1⅛"-thick stock when cut at a 45° bevel angle. This translates into more time for the cut and a thicker scroll saw blade for most effective cutting.

One exercise that can help you become familiar with bevel cutting is worthwhile. Begin by making a U shape on a short piece of ¾"-thick scrap wood. Draw the open end of the U at the end of the piece. Next, adjust the scroll saw table to about 6° and cut out the U shape, keeping the inside of the U

to the left of the blade, or on the low side of the table, as you make the cut.

After you make the cut, remove the wood from the saw and push the U shape through the waste. You will only be able to push part way, as the top of the cut will be wider than the bottom of the cut. You will also find that you have created a sunken U shape on one side of the board and a raised U shape on the other.

Determining the amount of tilt to the scroll saw table depends on how much you want the pattern to be raised or sunken, stock thickness, blade-kerf width, and detail in the pattern (greater detail means using a less acute angle for successful cutting). As a rule, it is always best to practice a given bevel

Simply disconnect the existing blower system and attach an aquarium pump to the tubing.

angle on scrap material before actually cutting out a project. Experiment with scrap material that is the same thickness as the material you will be using on the main project.

Sawdust Blower

It is probably safe to say that anyone who uses a scroll saw with any regularity will not be satisfied with the sawdust-blowing attachment that came on his or her saw. At least part of the problem stems from the fact that these units work on a small bellows that is operated by the lower arm of the saw. While the blower may work marginally at high speeds—when the bellows is being pumped rap-

Make a custom sawdust blower with an aquarium pump, plastic tubing, and copper tubing for the tip. Make sure your installation does not interfere with your saw's operation.

idly—at lower saw speeds, any blower is almost useless.

Another problem with any installed sawdust-blowing system is that most units have a nozzle that points at the operator, so when the unit is working, the sawdust is blown at the user. At the very least this is annoying.

One very simple solution to this common problem involves the use of an aquarium pump. If your saw has clear plastic tubing for an existing blower system, simply disconnect this and attach it to the aquarium pump. You will also have to adjust the nozzle tip on your unit to blow the sawdust off to the side.

If your saw is not equipped with a sawdust blower (and many inexpensive, imported units do not have this feature), purchase several feet of clear plastic air line when you buy the aquarium pump. You will also require about 8 inches of $\frac{1}{4}''$-diameter copper tubing to make a nozzle for the end of the plastic tubing. Since this is a custom operation, you will have to fasten the plastic tubing and copper tip along the top of the scroll saw. Use hose clamps or duct tape for this. Next bend the copper tubing so it arches past the scroll saw blade and blows sawdust to the rear of the table. You may find it necessary to crimp the end of the tubing to increase air flow and make the tip more effective. In all cases, make certain that the system does not affect the operation of the scroll saw and that you have not created a problem for yourself when changing blades.

Scroll sawing is an enjoyable hobby that can be practiced by almost any member of the family and can provide a lifetime of exciting woodworking projects. In later chapters you will learn how to accomplish a variety of cuts as well as how to finish your projects so they look professionally made. Please always use your scroll saw safely to avoid mishap.

CHAPTER THREE
Making Children's Toys

This chair is designed for a small child (page 36).

Toys are fun and easy to make. They make good projects for beginners, and small children will love to play with them. In addition, you can easily make a variety of toys that don't cost a fortune and, unlike most toys found in stores, will last a long time, even when left outside.

Most of the toy projects in this chapter are designed for small children, so keep this in mind when tracing the patterns and cutting the projects out. Little children seem to love toys that are designed in miniature.

Elephant Crayon Holder

This fun project is great for a small child's desk or drawing table. This project makes a great Christmas gift or party favors for a group of kids. The basic unit holds five crayons but can be expanded to hold a few more if necessary. The basic shape can be cut quickly from scrap material—2 × 4 and 2 × 6 scraps work well, as the base will be more stable than if the project is made with thinner material.

1 Begin by scaling the pattern on a copy machine to about 3½″ high for 2 × 4 lumber or about 5½″ high for 2 × 6 lumber.

2 Next, transfer the pattern to the scrap lumber— either trace the pattern using carbon paper or use spray adhesive to attach the pattern directly to the wood.

3 Cut out the elephant with a coarse blade—9 to 12 teeth-per-inch—beginning with the foot detail. Then cut out the front of the body and the trunk, working around the head toward the tail.

4 After cutting, bore five holes (each ¼″ in diameter) evenly spaced along the back. These holes work for standard size crayons; if your child uses larger crayons, enlarge the hole sizes accordingly. The holes should be about 2″ deep.

Elephant Crayon Holder Pattern

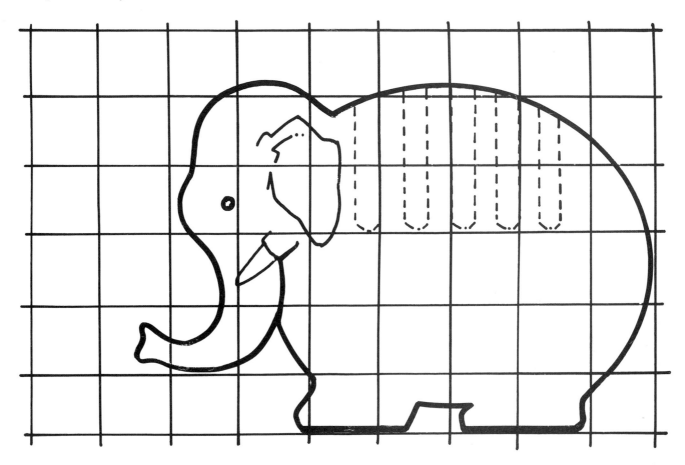

Materials Required

Scrap 2 × 4 or 2 × 6 lumber

Bright enamel paint

Time required: ½ hour

Scaling: 2 × 4—95%; 2 × 6—145%

Elephant Crayon Holder

5 Finish the elephant by sanding all edges and applying two coats of any brightly colored, gloss enamel paint. Once these coats dry add eye, tusk, ear, mouth and trunk detail—use waterproof marker, India ink or paint.

This project is so easy you will probably want to make several at a time.

Duck Stacking Toy

Stacking toys are popular with small children and get hours of use. This is an easy project for beginners to make and one that just may see more use than the plastic versions commonly found in toy stores. This project has a duck's head, but you can, of course, change it to have no head at all—toddlers don't seem to care.

1 Begin by marking the lumber with a compass. You will need seven circles, including the base, as follows: (2) 4½", 4", 3½", 3", 2½ and 2".

2 Next, trace the head pattern on the lumber. Cut out all pieces on a scroll saw using a coarse blade (9 to 12 teeth-per-inch).

3 Now bore a ¾" hole through the center of all disks (except the base); drill a ¾" hole halfway through the base disk. Bore a ¾" hole ½" into the bottom of the duck's head.

4 Sand all edges and around the rims of all holes (except the base). This sanding will allow the disks to pass over the dowel and stack easier.

5 The duck head can be carved or sanded to give it more definition. Do not remove too much material, however, as this will increase the chances of it breaking over time.

6 Next, finish each disk in a different color. Bright enamels look good and are appealing to small children. Bright-colored stains can also be used effectively. Paint the duck head green with a yellow bill, and paint in the eyes. Finally, glue the dowel into the base. Allow to dry before use.

Materials Required

1 × 6 × 24"—hardwood or softwood

5" of ¾" wooden dowel

Time required: 2 hours

Stacking Duck Pattern

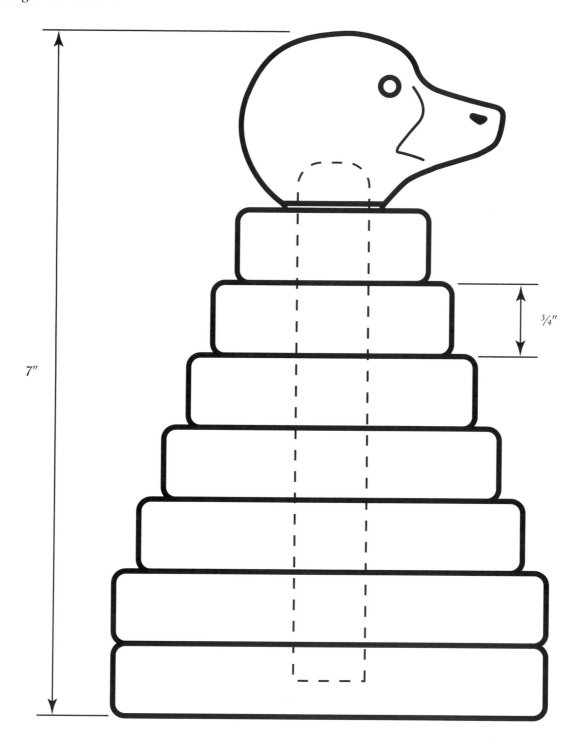

7"

3/4"

Child's Chair

This chair project, sized just right for youngsters from two to six years old, is an ideal woodworking project for beginners as there are no complicated woodworking joints. The chair is simple to make, will delight any child, and costs less than ten dollars for all materials. Children love to sit in a chair that is their size, and the heart-shaped hole in the back makes carrying and moving easy for small hands.

The basic design of the chair lends itself well to modification, or you can duplicate its worthwhile lines as is. The wide base offered by 1 × 12 lumber ensures stability. The pattern shown was designed with a round top and indented sides. The round top is safer for small children than a flat or pointed edge. The indented sides add a little flair and, of possible greater importance, also lighten the chair so that it can easily be moved around by young children. In this case, form does indeed follow function.

1 Begin by cutting the pieces to length as indicated in the materials list. Next, on a scroll saw, cut out the pieces, including the heart-shaped hole in the back.

2 After all pieces have been cut out, sand all surfaces thoroughly, including the edges and heart-shaped hole. Sand with the grain, using 200 or finer grit paper.

The importance of flat edges for tight woodworking joints is really tested when assembling furniture, especially when the piece is designed to be moved by small children. Unfortunately, the easiest woodworking joints to make are not the strongest. All of the joints in this chair are simple butt joints—flat mating surfaces—and are adequate. If your woodworking skills and tools are more advanced, you might want to make the seatback joint a dado joint for added strength. A dado groove approximately ⅜″ deep in the seat back will make the chair much stronger. To do this, cut the seat (see materials list) 9⅜″ long, and make a dado cut ⅜″ deep at the proper location in the seat back.

Materials Required

1—6′ length of 1 × 12 pine, cut as follows:

Back—24″ long

Seat—9″ long

Front—8″ long

Brace—8 × 3″

Woodworking glue

Finish nails (#6)

3 Assemble the chair pieces using woodworking glue and #6 finishing nails. Countersink the nail heads and fill the holes with wood putty or other suitable filler. It is usually best to fill the nail holes twice, sanding between applications.

4 Sand the entire chair with 200-grit paper prior to coating with wood primer.

After the primer dries, sand lightly and apply a coat of finish paint. When this dries, sand again and apply a second and final coat of finish paint.

5 For a truly custom look, trace a decorative pattern on the seat back and front. Draw the pattern freehand or use stencils, which are readily available at craft supply stores. Paint the pattern using an artist's brush and acrylic paints.

6 Once the design dries, spray the entire chair with a clear coating such as Krylon—this will make the chair easy to wipe clean. Allow the chair to dry thoroughly before use.

One variation to this chair project is to use an attractive wood, such as redwood or maple, and finish with varnish or polyurethane. The clear finish will bring out the natural beauty of the wood. A stencil overlay, utilizing suitable colors, works well over natural wood tones.

This simple chair will delight any child and should provide years of use.

Child's Chair Pattern

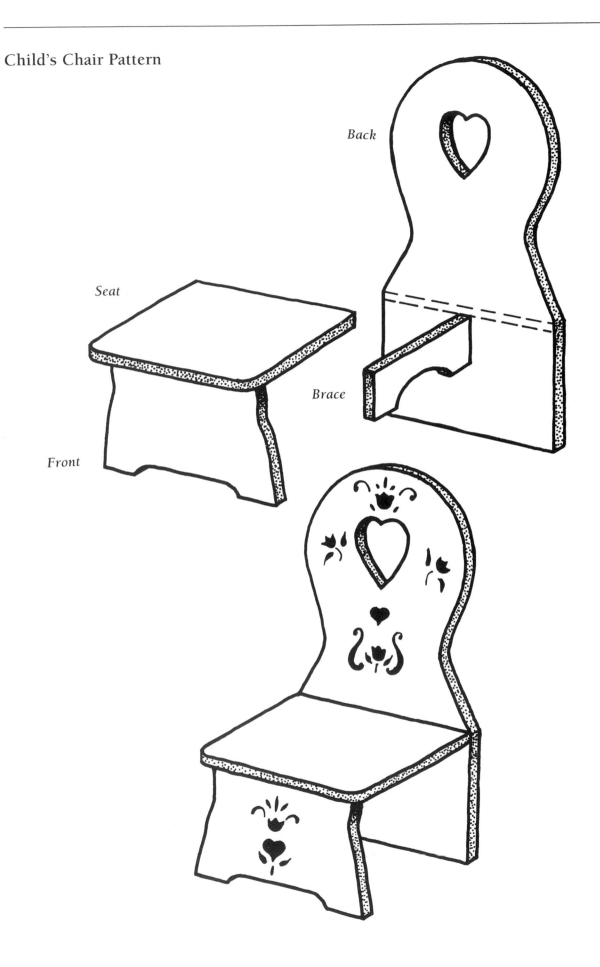

Back

Seat

Brace

Front

Rocking Horse

This fun project—easily constructed in a few hours from materials you probably have lying around the workshop—is a durable toy that can last for generations. If you are using ¾″ lumber, lay out the pattern so the grain runs lengthwise on both the seat and rockers. When laying out the head, the grain should run from the ears to the nose. If you are using cabinet grade plywood, simply trace the pattern so the surface grain runs lengthwise on all pieces. Keep in mind that this project will be stronger if you use ¾″ lumber for the seat and rockers and plywood for the head.

1 Begin by enlarging the pattern on a copy machine (the grid system consists of 1″ squares). Next, transfer the pattern to the lumber you will be using for the project. Trace the pattern using carbon paper, or attach it directly to the lumber using spray adhesive.

2 Carefully cut out the pieces on your scroll saw using a suitable blade. Cut the seat brace and the hardwood dowel. After the pieces have been cut, mark the location of the dowel handle and bore a ⅜″ hole.

3 Next, mark the location of the screws and bore holes here as well. Countersink the screw holes so the screwheads will be below the surface when installed.

4 Sanding is the next step; you should spend at least as much time at this task as in cutting the pieces. Keep in mind the fact that every square inch of this rocking horse will be handled by a toddler—all surfaces should be as smooth as possible. In addition to sanding all flat surfaces, spend some time sanding all edges so they are slightly rounded. Use progressively finer grades of sandpaper until the project is as smooth as glass.

5 Before assembling the project, draw the head detail using a pen and India ink or waterproof markers. Next, paint the details using suitably colored

---

Materials Required

Seat (1)—¾ × 10½ × 16″ pine, hardwood or cabinet grade plywood

Rockers (2)—¾ × 4 × 16″ pine, hardwood or cabinet grade plywood

Head (1)—¾ × 9 × 11″ pine, hardwood or cabinet grade plywood

Seat brace (1)—¾ × 2 × 3½″ pine or hardwood

Handle (1)—5″ of ⅜″ hardwood dowel

No. 8 × 1¼″ flathead wood screws

Wood plugs or hole filler (screwhead covers)

Woodworking glue

Acrylic paints and colored markers

Clear finish

Time required: 4 hours

One square = 1″

Finish Materials Required

Filler for nail holes

Wood primer

Gloss enamel

Stencil and acrylic paints

Clear coating spray

Time required: 3 hours

---

acrylic paints: eyes, white and blue; halter, red; mane, blonde, brown or black. Allow the paint to dry before putting parts together.

6 Begin assembly by locating the rockers under the seat and fastening from above with No. 8 × 1¼″ wood screws. You will find this easier to do if you predrill through the rockers and the seat. Apply a bead of woodworking glue between the seat and the tops of the rockers for added strength. Be sure to countersink the screwheads by tightening fully. Next, attach the seat brace using woodworking glue and No. 8 × 1¼″ wood screws. Wipe away any excess glue with a damp rag.

Rocking Horse Pattern

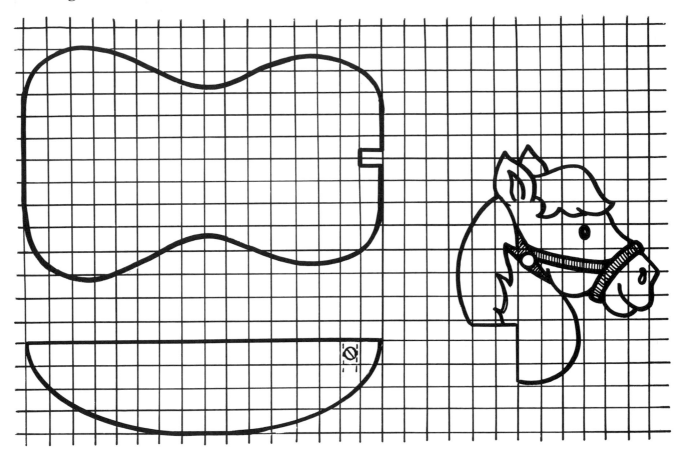

7 Fasten the head in place in the notch in the seat with woodworking glue and No. 8 × 1¼″ wood screws driven up from under the seat and through the back of the seat brace.

8 Next, fill all countersunk screw holes with either wooden plugs or wood putty. Sand the plugs immediately; allow the putty to harden before sanding.

9 Apply a bead of woodworking glue to the dowel hole in the horse's head and push the dowel into place so it is of equal length on either side of the head. Wipe away any excess glue with a damp rag.

10 After all glue has set (about two hours), apply several coats of clear finish to the entire project rocker, lightly sanding with steel wool between coats. Allow each coat of the clear finish to dry thoroughly

Rocking Horse Assembly Diagram.

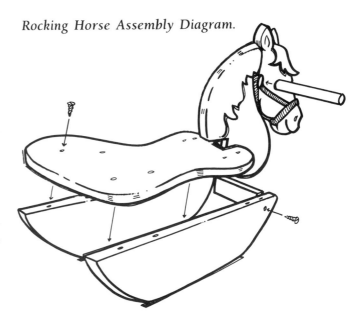

before applying additional coats.

Once the final clear coat has dried, this rocking horse is ready for service.

Dinosaur Bank

This fun project makes a great gift with an added bonus—it encourages saving.

1 Begin by making a copy of this full-size pattern on a copy machine. Next, transfer the pattern to the lumber, making sure the grain is running vertically. Either trace the pattern directly to the lumber or attach the pattern to the lumber using spray adhesive. Also transfer the two feet to the 1 × 4 pine. Last, trace the circles on a sheet of Plexiglas (you will need two 3½″ circles). To prevent splitting or splintering of the Plexiglas, cover both sides with masking tape and trace the circle on top.

2 Begin by cutting the dinosaur body. Use a coarse (9 teeth-per-inch) blade for this cutting. Next, drill a pilot hole for threading the scroll saw blade, and then cut out a 2¾″ circle as indicated. Cut the feet next, using a suitable blade. Last, cut the Plexiglas circles. You will find the cutting easier if you use a coarse blade (about 9 teeth-per-inch) and don't try to force the cutting.

3 Next, you must drill a series of ⅛″ holes through the shoulder area for the coin slot. After the holes have been drilled, square off the slot with a wood rasp or file. Check how the slot works by dropping coins into it. If the coins hang up, enlarge the hole or make the interior smoother with a file.

Materials Required

1—2 × 8 × 9″ dimensional lumber
2—feet cut from 1 × 4 pine
2—3½″ disks cut from ⅛″ Plexiglas
8—½″-long roundheaded brass wood screws
4—1½″ flathead wood screws (for attaching the feet)
Suitable paints, clear coating and markers
Time required: 1 hour

4 Before assembly, finish the dinosaur. Begin by sanding all parts smooth with 200-grit sandpaper. Next, paint the body and feet green and the teeth white. Then draw the eyes and teeth with a waterproof felt-tip pen or India ink. Finally, when all paints are dry, apply two or more coats of clear finish.

5 After the clear finish is dry, attach the Plexiglas disks to both sides of the dinosaur as indicated in the pattern. Finally, attach the feet. First, predrill two countersunk holes in each foot. Attach each foot with a spot of woodworking glue and two screws.

Dinosaur Bank Pattern

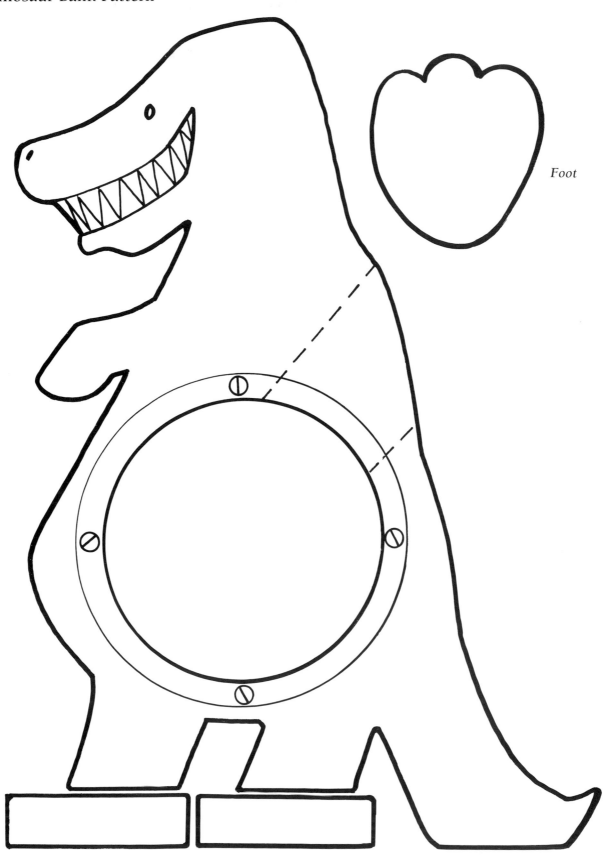

Foot

Mini Dinosaurs

Mini dinosaurs are designed to be played with by small children. These wooden toys can be used indoors or out and will provide hours of creative play. They are extremely easy to make—simply trace the pattern and cut out on a scroll saw. They can be left natural (no finish), painted, or clear coated with polyurethane or linseed oil.

Softwoods, such as white pine or redwood, are easy to work and look quite good. Maple, walnut, oak and other hardwoods don't cut as easily, but the natural colors often create interesting looking dinosaurs.

1 Begin by copying the pattern on a copy machine. The size shown works well, but it can also be enlarged or reduced. However, if you plan to give these to children three years of age or younger, it's best not to reduce the pattern sizes too much. Small parts will present a choking hazard to young children.

2 Transfer the pattern using carbon paper or attach the photocopy directly to the stock. Lay out the pattern to take best advantage of the grain. As a general rule, the grain should run the length of the dinosaur.

Materials Required

1 × 4 and 1 × 6 solid scrap lumber, hardwood or softwood

Semigloss paint or clear coating

Time required: 5 minutes each

3 Cut out the pattern using the scroll saw.

4 Sand all surfaces thoroughly, taking particular care to smooth and soften any sharp edges. In addition to making the toys safer, rounded edges will accept a finish better.

5 Several finishing options are available. For a natural look, they can be left unfinished. Or, a couple of coats of polyurethane can be added to provide a clear, smooth, easier-to-clean finish. Since children love colors, consider a bright enamel paint—just make sure it's nontoxic when dry. Good color choices include bright green, yellow, red and brown. Once the paint dries, add eye details with a pen and India ink or a waterproof marker.

Mini Dinosaurs Patterns

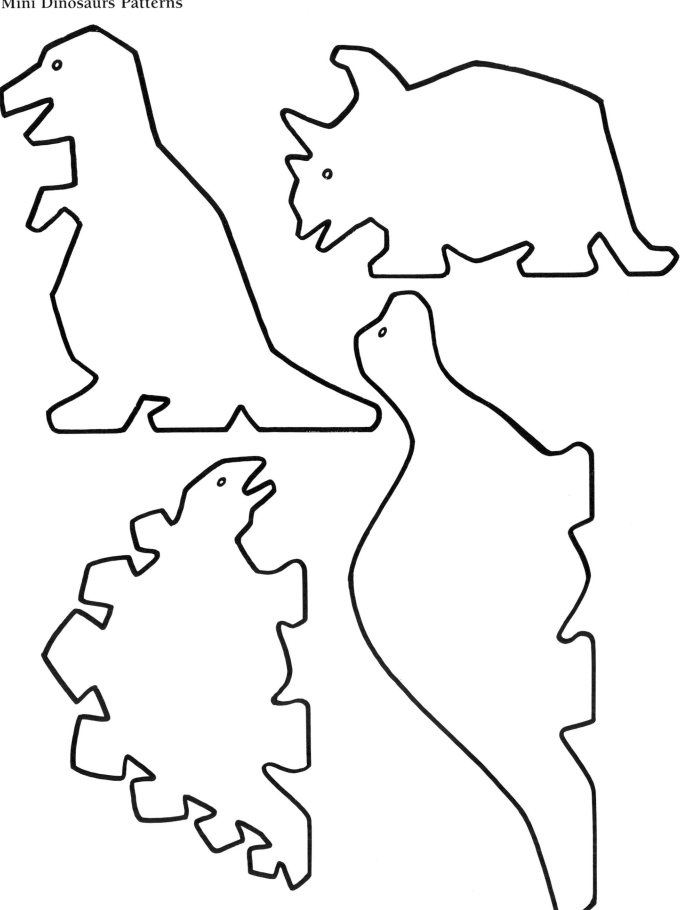

Stick Pony

This has got to be one of the simplest scroll saw projects to make but one that will delight any small child. It is sure to see hours of use and can easily be passed down from one toddler to another. One thing to keep in mind is that the lighter the material used for the head, the better. Cabinet grade plywood is a bit heavy and will tend to make this stick pony unbalanced. White pine is a good choice. The stick itself is ½" wooden dowel, which is a good size for small hands.

1 Begin by enlarging the basic pattern on a copy machine. As a guideline, the squares are 1", but this can be varied slightly. Transfer the pattern to the lumber either by tracing over carbon paper or by using spray adhesive to attach the pattern directly.

2 Cut the head outline using a suitable blade on the scroll saw. Next, drill a ½" × 2" hole as indicated in the diagram. Last, cut the ½" wooden dowel to length.

3 Next, turn your attention to finishing the head. Begin by thoroughly sanding all edges and surfaces. Use progressively lighter grits of sandpaper for this. Round all edges slightly. Sand the wooden dowel until it is smooth.

4 To finish, begin by painting the entire head light brown. Then, once this coat dries, transfer the mane, halter, eyes, nose, ears and teeth patterns using

Materials Required

Head—¾ × 12 × 12" white pine or plywood

Stick—36" length of ½" dowel

Suitable acrylic paints, marker or India ink

Clear coating

Time required: 2 hours

One square = 1"

either India ink and a pen or a waterproof felt-tip marker. Next, paint the detail of these features using suitable colors of acrylic paints. For example, paint the mane blonde or black, the eyes white and blue, the teeth white, and the halter red or brown. After these paints dry, apply two coats of a clear finish, sanding lightly with steel wool between coats. Also apply two coats of clear finish to the stick, but avoid finishing the portion of the stick that will fit into the hole (woodworking glue doesn't adhere well to finishes).

5 The final step is to attach the stick to the head. To do this, coat one end of the dowel with woodworking glue and press the stick into the hole in the horse's neck. Twist to ensure a good bond; allow the glue to set up overnight. The next morning, this pony is ready for a ride.

Stick Pony Pattern

Alphabet Letters

The letters in this section are not intended to be a project themselves as much as part of other projects—two such projects, Personalized Hat/Coat Rack and Initialed Book Rack, follow this section. You can, of course, use these letters for any project that requires lettering.

When designing a project with lettering, use a copy machine to help you make templates that suit your size requirements.

Materials Required

Hardwood

Softwood

Plywood

Plexiglas

Sheet metals

Alphabet Letters

A B C D E

F G H I J

K L M N O

P Q R S T

U V W X Y Z

Numbers and Upper/Lower Case

1 2 3 4 5 6

7 8 9 0

a b c d e

f g h i j k

l m n o p

q r s t u

v w x y z

Initialed Book Rack

Young children love things that are personalized with their initials, so this book rack is a natural that is sure to be popular. A wide range of wood materials can be used to make this book rack, and each has its advantages and disadvantages. Solid lumber requires little edge finishing other than sanding and coating with paint or stain, followed by a clear finish. But solid stock can present a problem when used to make certain letters. Those letters with long, narrow legs (letters *E*, *F*, *P*, *T*, *V* and *Y*, for example) will have considerable short-grain, which can easily break off if the project is bumped or dropped.

Plywood, with its laminated cross-grain construction, doesn't have the same short-grain problem as solid stock, so it's more likely to survive a nasty knock. However, plywood requires a good deal of filling and sanding in order to get acceptably smooth edges.

1 Begin making an initialed book rack by choosing the letter or letters you plan to use. Enlarge these letters on a copy machine so each letter is approximately 6″ wide and about 8″ high.

2 Next, transfer the pattern to solid stock or plywood using either carbon paper for tracing or spray adhesive for direct attachment of the pattern.

3 Next, cut out the letter(s) for the book rack using a scroll saw and a suitable blade. For letters with a cutout—such as *O*, *B* or *P*—drill a pilot hole inside the letter for threading the saw blade, then make the cutout. Next, cut the base to length (16″).

4 After cutting, sand the letter(s) smooth both on the faces and around the edges. Some areas—the

---

Materials Required

2—¾ × 8 × 9″ hardwood, softwood or plywood (for letters)
1—½ × 8 × 16″ hardwood, softwood or plywood (for base)
4—1″ flathead wood screws
Woodworking glue
4—½″ wood plugs, or wood putty for filling screw holes
Paint or stain and clear finish
Time required: 2 hours

---

center of the letter *V*, for example—can be difficult to sand by conventional means. For such areas, try wrapping sandpaper around a small wooden dowel or use an emery board. An electric spindle sander also works well for this type of sanding.

If you are using plywood, special edge treatment must be used. Basically there are two choices: You can fill the edges with putty and sand smooth when dry, or you can apply several coats of paint to fill the edges.

5 After sanding is complete, attach the letters to the base of the book rack. To do this, begin by drilling countersunk pilot holes from the underside of the base. Place the letter in position so you can mark exactly where to drill. Attach the letters—one at each end—using two wood screws and woodworking glue. Last, fill the screw holes with either wooden plugs or wood putty. Sand smooth. You will need to file a flat area on the round bottom edges of the letters *C*, *G*, *S* and *U*.

6 Next, the book rack must be finished. It can be stained and clear coated, or painted. Once the paint dries, this book rack is ready for use on a desk or bookshelf.

Initialed Book Rack Pattern

Personalized Hat/Coat Rack

A possible solution for some of the clutter in a child's room is to make this hat/coat rack to encourage the child to hang up clothes, hats and coats. Because this rack is personalized, the child just might be reminded that the pegs below have a definite purpose. One good alternative to a child's name is simply the word *COATS*.

While this project can easily be made from any suitable solid wood, plywood will hold up better, especially when some of the more fragile letters (*E*, *F*, *P*, *T*, *V* and *Y*) are in a name. This is a simple project to complete but does require care when cutting the individual letters.

1 Begin by enlarging the required letters on a copy machine until each is 5″ high. Lay out the pattern on a sheet of plywood, leaving 4″ below the name.

2 Next, transfer the pattern using either carbon paper for tracing or spray adhesive for direct attachment of the pattern.

3 Cut out the individual letters in the name using a coarse reverse-tooth blade (about 9 teeth-per-inch). The reverse-tooth blade will minimize tear-out on the bottom side of the plywood. For letters with a cutout—such as *O*, *B* or *P*—drill a pilot hole inside the letter for threading the blade, then make the cutout.

4 After the name has been cut out, bore ¹/₂″ holes 3¹/₂″ apart and about 2″ up from the bottom. Bore a minimum of four holes, more for a longer name. Before installing the pegs, sand all surfaces of the rack. If desired, you can fill the edges of the plywood with wood putty. Allow the putty to dry before the final sanding.

5 Next, cut the required number of dowels, each 3¾″ long. Sand the dowels and round off the ends that will protrude from the rack. Install each of the dowels using woodworking glue.

Materials Required

¾″ A/B interior plywood—large enough for a child's name in 5″ letters and a 4″ rack below

4—3¾″ lengths of ½″ wooden dowels

Paint or stain and clear coating

Mounting screws for attaching to wall

Time required: 2 hours

6 Finish the rack with paint or stain. If stain is used, follow it with two coats of clear finish. Last, hang the rack in a suitable location. This can be accomplished by screwing directly through the rack into wall studs. To make this rack more useful, check the reach of the child who will be using the rack and hang at this level.

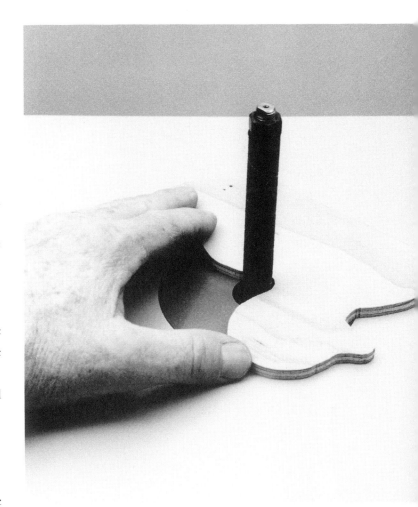

A spindle sander is very handy for sanding shapes.

Personalized Hat/Coat Rack Pattern

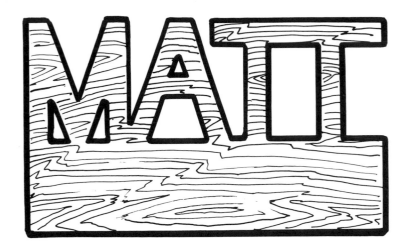

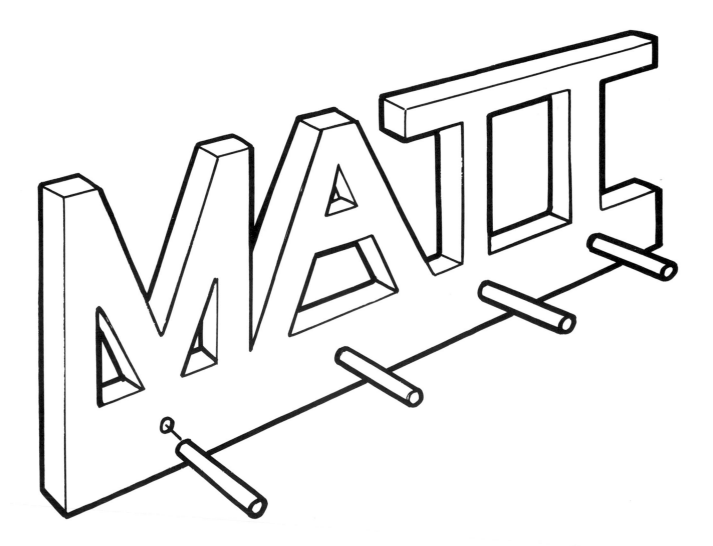

CHAPTER FOUR
Decorative Shelves

Decorative shelves are easy to make on a scroll saw and do not require much material—most can be made with about one square foot of material. With the exception of the first shelf project, all of the other projects in this chapter are designed to be made from softwood, hardwood or plywood that is ¼" thick. Probably the easiest to work with is hardwood-faced ¼" plywood. Another benefit of plywood is that it is more durable and easier to work with than solid wood because the grain pattern is not a major factor in laying out the pattern.

Selecting Stock

When using plywood for a decorative shelf, A/B grade can be used for the back, but A/A grade should be used for both the shelf and shelf support as both sides of these parts will be visible. As an alternative, you can use ¼" solid wood for both the shelf and support bracket. If you use solid wood, try to select stock that matches the color and grain of the plywood back.

Some of the better choices for plywood include oak, birch, walnut, cherry, mahogany and teak. Avoid fir and lauan plywoods, as these splinter easily when cutting and do not finish as well as other types.

Of course, solid wood can be used for any shelf project in this chapter if available in ¼" thicknesses. Solid woods are a good choice for patterns that do not have a lot of intricate detail. In addition, solid wood shelves look great when finished with two coats of a clear finish. Some of the better choices of hardwood that look great with a natural finish include soft maple, oak, cherry, walnut, birch and mahogany. If the shelf will be painted, pine, poplar and basswood are good choices and easy to work with.

1 Begin by duplicating the patterns on a copier. The patterns are actual size, so enlargement or reduction is not required. Cut along the dotted lines and fasten the two pieces together with tape. This project requires two sides and one shelf.

2 Lay out the patterns on the stock (hardwood, softwood or plywood) with the grain running vertically for the two side pieces and across the shelf from flat side to flat side.

3 Next, transfer the patterns to the stock using either carbon paper for tracing or spray adhesive to attach the pattern directly.

4 Now cut the parts on a scroll saw fitted with a blade suitable for the material you are cutting. Work slowly and cut along the pattern lines carefully.

Solid Corner Shelf

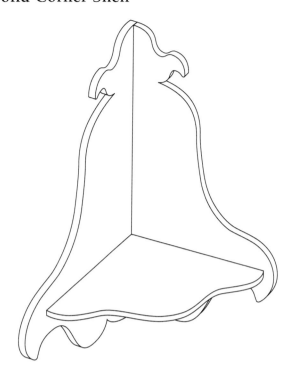
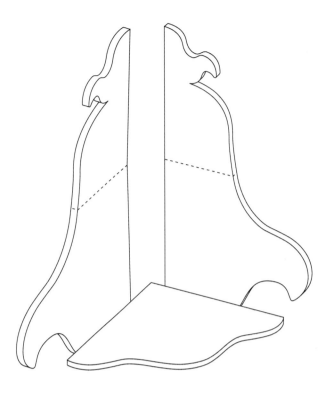

Materials Required

Hardwood, softwood or hardwood-faced A/A grade plywood

1—⅜ × 6⅜ × 12″ (shelf side)

1—⅜ × 6 × 12″ (shelf side)

1—⅜ × 6 × 6″ (shelf)

Woodworking glue

9—#4 finish nails

Paint or stain and/or clear finish

Time required: 2 hours

Keep in mind that for ⅜″ stock, one side must be ⅜″ narrower than the other side so that they overlap and can be nailed.

5 After both sides and the shelf have been cut to your satisfaction, sand the faces of the side pieces and both sides of the shelf. Round the edges slightly with sandpaper if desired. Remove any saw marks around the edges with sandpaper or power-sanding equipment.

6 Next, assemble the corner shelf using #4 finish nails and woodworking glue. Begin by attaching the two side pieces together. Apply a bead of woodworking glue along both mating surfaces, align the edges so they are square, and then drive four or five finishing nails through the back piece into the edge of the front piece.

7 Next, position the shelf about 3¼″ up from the bottom and mark this location. Apply woodworking glue to the mating surfaces and fasten the shelf from the back with finish nails.

8 Now the shelf can be finished with paint or stain and clear finish. If painting, it is always preferable to apply several light coats rather than one or two heavy coats. If staining, wipe the stain on using a clean, soft cloth. Do not apply too heavy a coat of stain, and wipe up any excess stain after a few minutes. Once the stain dries, apply two coats of clear finish—shellac, varnish or polyurethane—allowing the first coat to dry before applying the second coat.

Solid Shelf Pattern

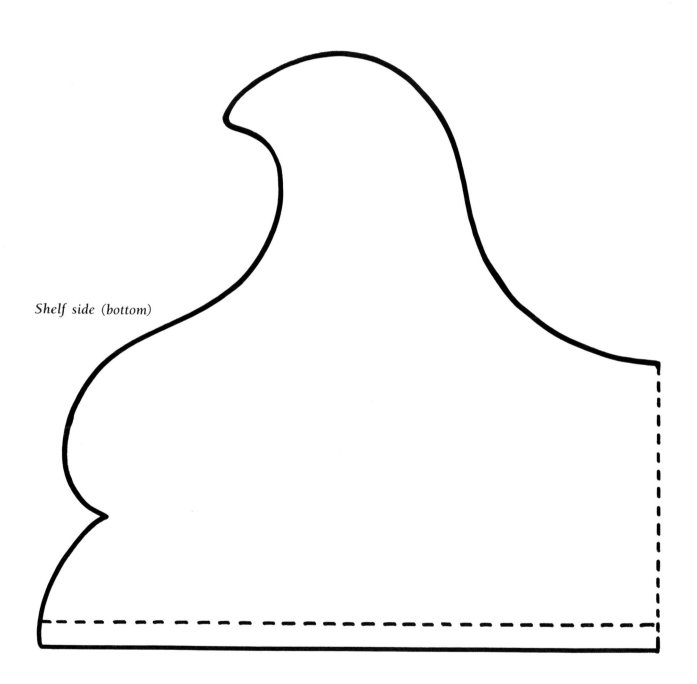

Shelf side (bottom)

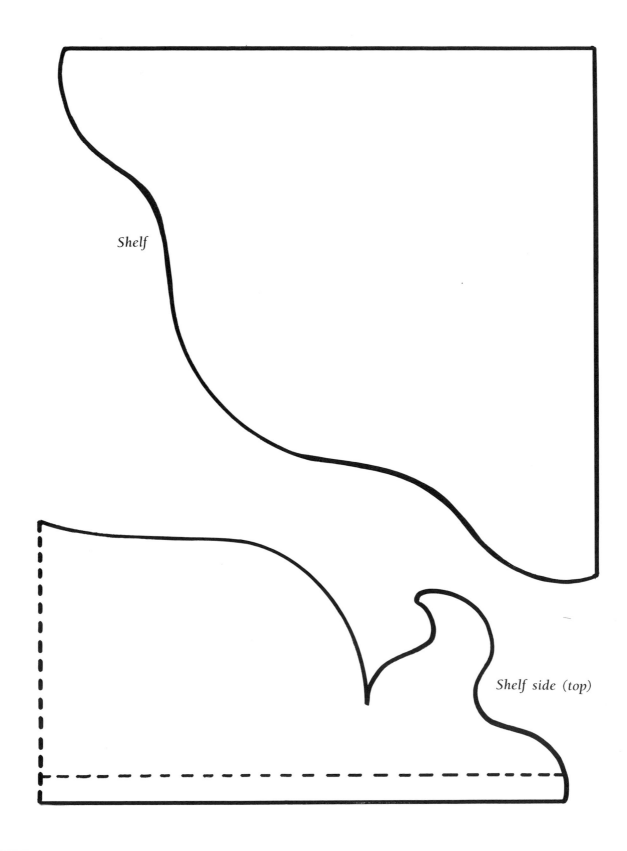

Shelf

Shelf side (top)

Four Fretwork Shelves

The four fretwork shelves that follow are all fairly simple to make and will look good on any wall. Some general comments may help with any shelf and are therefore worthwhile passing along at this point.

If you are planning to make more than one shelf, consider stack sawing the parts. See chapter two for a description of how to do this.

Drill Pilot Holes

When drilling saw gates—pilot holes for the scroll saw blade—bore the hole away from the cut line whenever possible. Then thread the blade through the hole, cut to the pattern line, and begin cutting out the detail. When making the pilot hole, use a piece of scrap lumber under the workpiece—this will minimize splintering of the area around the pilot hole.

Assemble the Patterns

You will notice that all of the shelf patterns in this chapter cover at least two pages. This was done because of space limitations. Each pattern—when copied and joined to other elements of the shelf—is a full-size shelf. You may find it easiest to first copy the pattern, cut along the indicated dotted lines, assemble the full pattern with tape, then copy the full pattern before use. Of course, you can enlarge any pattern on a copy machine to make it larger than the size offered.

This decorative shelf will look good on any wall.

Use a block of scrap lumber under the workpiece when drilling pilot holes to minimize tear-out by the drill bit.

Assemble the pattern parts after copying; this will make tracing the pattern on the workpiece much easier.

Pneumatic nailers are very handy for joining decorative shelves and other woodworking projects.

Transfer the Patterns

When transferring patterns, use one of two methods: carbon paper tracing or direct application of the pattern to the workpiece. To quickly review these two methods, you can easily transfer a shelf pattern by using carbon paper and a round-pointed pencil (a sharp pencil point tends to tear the pattern). Hold the pattern on the workpiece with tape, push-pins or staples.

Spray adhesive can also be used to attach a pattern directly to the workpiece. Lightly spray the adhesive on the back of the paper pattern—not the wood—wait a few seconds for the adhesive to become tacky, then apply the pattern to the workpiece. Smooth with your hand to remove any air bubbles and you are ready for cutting. After the pattern has been cut out, simply peel off the pattern. Spray adhesive does not usually leave any residue, but the surface should always be lightly sanded before applying any type of finish.

Sand

Sand all parts of your shelf project before assembly. It is much easier to sand flat pieces than it is to sand a project that has been put together. If necessary, fill the edges of plywood with wood putty or wood filler. Allow this to dry hard before sanding.

Assemble

When assembling any shelf, use both woodworking glue and wire brads at least 5/8″ long. As a rule, it is best to predrill nail holes with a suitable size drill bit. If you don't have the right size drill bit—it should be slightly smaller than the brad—simply clip the head off a brad and use it as a drill bit.

As a good alternative to nailing with brads, consider using a pneumatic stapler or brad nailer. The benefits of pneumatic tools are unknown to many do-it-yourselfers but well understood by professionals. While a discussion of pneumatic tools is beyond the scope of this book, using such tools for fastening woodworking projects makes sense.

Apply a light coat of woodworking glue to all mating surfaces after predrilling nail holes. Carefully wipe off any excess glue that oozes out between the pieces with a damp cloth. This is really important if the project will be stained or clear finished, as glue will not take a stain.

Always wipe off excess woodworking glue with a damp rag before it hardens.

Hanging the Shelves

There are basically three ways to attach any of these shelf projects to a wall. The first method is to drill two pilot holes through the back of the shelf and screw the shelf to the wall. If possible, drive at least one of the screws into a wall stud; if not, use hollow wall fasteners, such as small toggle bolts. The second method is to drive two finish nails at suitable locations and simply hang the shelf through the decora-tive fretwork. Once again, drive at least one of the nails into a wall stud. The third method of shelf attachment utilizes a special brass hanger—there are several types available at woodworking and hardware stores. In most cases, a single hanger attached to the top of the shelf will be more than sufficient to hold the shelf.

This brass hanger is one way to hang a decorative shelf.

Fretwork Shelf #1

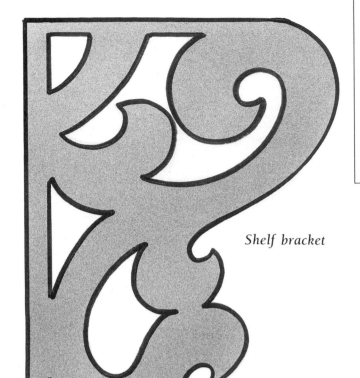

Shelf bracket

Shelf

Materials Required

Back (1)—¼ × 10½ × 7½″ hardwood, softwood or plywood

Shelf bracket (1)—¼ × 3½ × 5″ hardwood, softwood or plywood

Shelf (1)—¼ × 3¾ × 7″ hardwood, softwood or plywood

Woodworking glue

Wire brads—⅝″ minimum

Paint or stain and clear finish

Time required: 2 hours

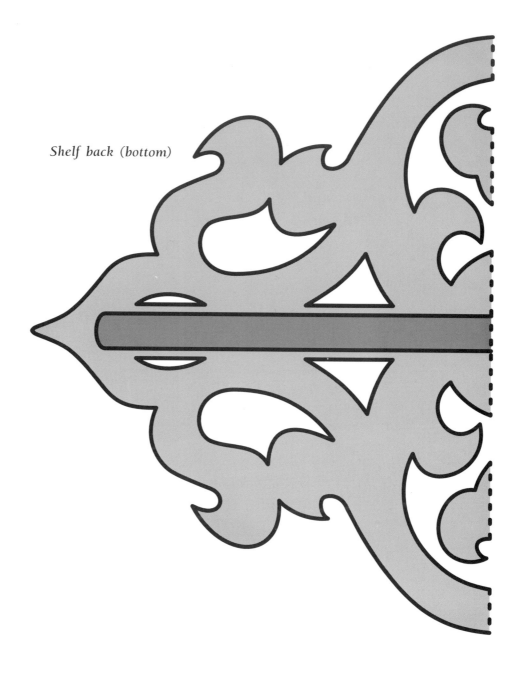

Shelf back (bottom)

Shelf back (top)

Fretwork Shelf #2

Materials Required

Back (1)—¼ × 13 × 8″ hardwood, softwood or plywood

Shelf bracket (1)—¼ × 4½ × 4½″ hardwood, softwood or plywood

Shelf (1)—¼ × 3½ × 7″ hardwood, softwood or plywood

Woodworking glue

Wire brads—⅝″ minimum

Paint or stain and clear finish

Time required: 2 hours

Shelf back (top)

Shelf back (bottom)

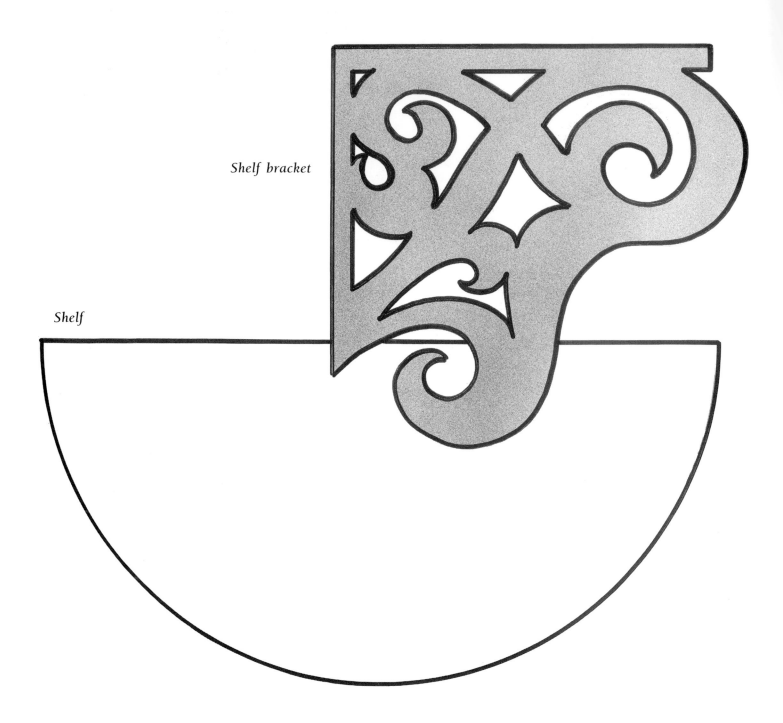

Shelf bracket

Shelf

Fretwork Shelf #3

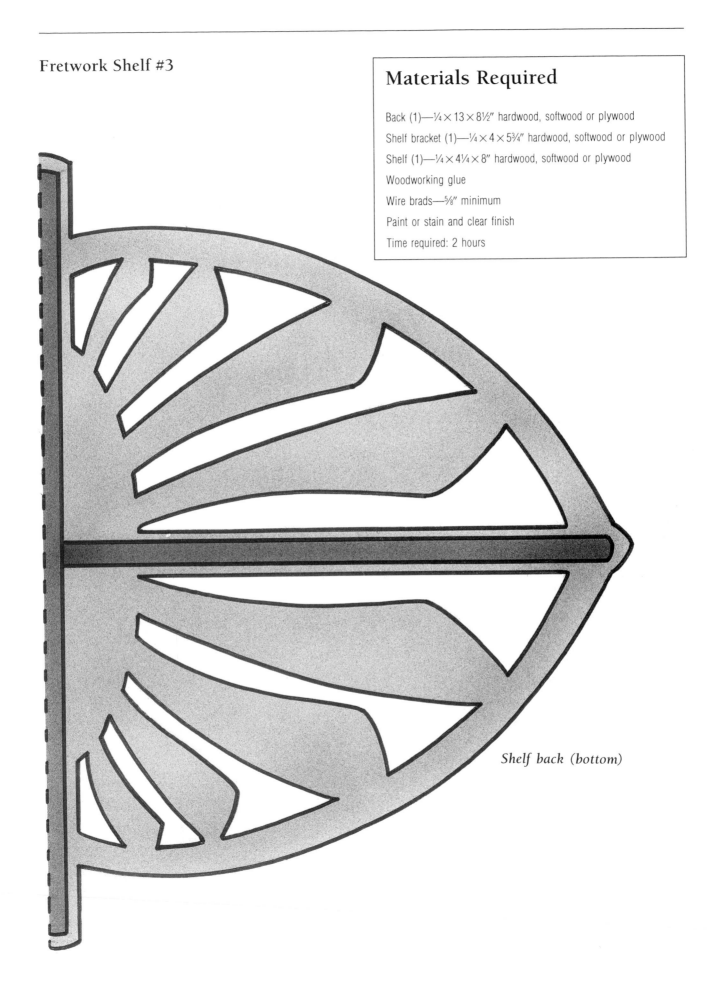

Materials Required

Back (1)—¼ × 13 × 8½″ hardwood, softwood or plywood

Shelf bracket (1)—¼ × 4 × 5¾″ hardwood, softwood or plywood

Shelf (1)—¼ × 4¼ × 8″ hardwood, softwood or plywood

Woodworking glue

Wire brads—⅝″ minimum

Paint or stain and clear finish

Time required: 2 hours

Shelf back (bottom)

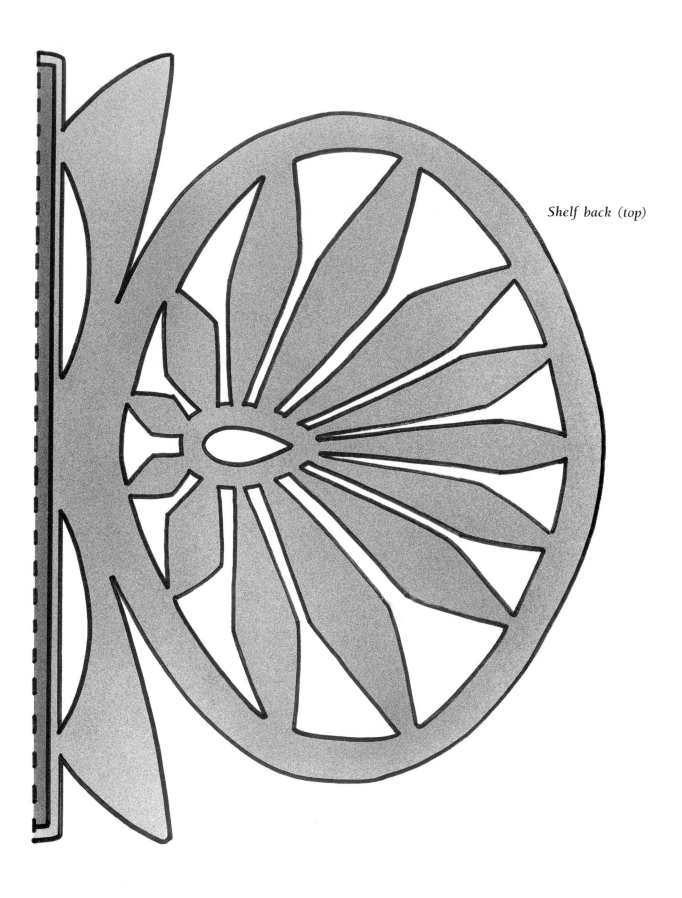

Shelf back (top)

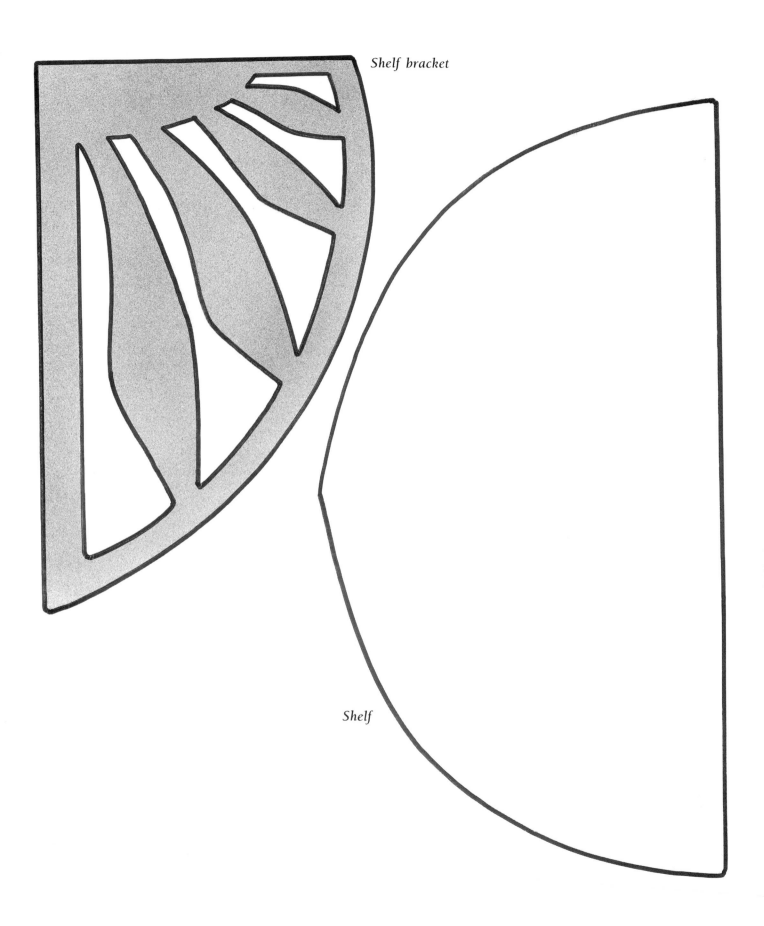

Shelf bracket

Shelf

Fretwork Shelf #4

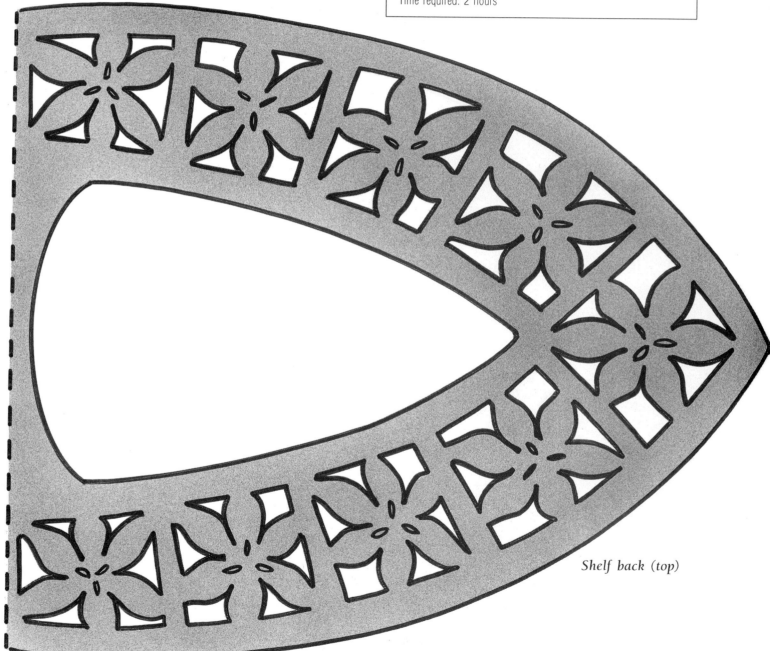

Materials Required

Back (1)—¼ × 6¾ × 11½″ hardwood, softwood or plywood

Shelf bracket (1)—¼ × 1½ × 2″ hardwood, softwood or plywood

Shelf (1)—¼ × 2 × 3¼″ hardwood, softwood or plywood

Woodworking glue

Wire brads—⅝″ minimum

Paint or stain and clear finish

Time required: 2 hours

Shelf back (top)

Shelf bracket

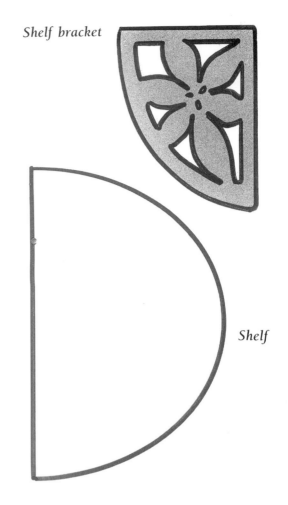

Shelf

Shelf back (bottom)

CHAPTER FIVE
Making Puzzles

Puzzles are fun projects to make on a scroll saw and can provide a creative way to spend an hour or two in the workshop. Puzzles are also a great way to use up some scrap material that you have been saving. As an added benefit, once they are made, puzzles will provide hours of fun time for the youngsters who will play with them.

Because puzzles make great gifts, some woodworkers have taken this a step further and turned an enjoyable pastime into a profitable side business.

All puzzles are either board or stand-alone types.

Handmade puzzles are popular items at art fairs, craft shops, flea markets, bazaars and gift shops. Making puzzles is a great way for anyone with a little skill on a scroll saw to turn a hobby into a means of extra income.

The puzzle designs offered in this chapter are intended to get you started on puzzle making. They fall into two broad categories: board puzzles and stand-alone puzzles.

All of the patterns are simple to make and require little in the way of materials—in fact, you probably have enough scrap lumber lying around your workshop to make many puzzles. Once you have mastered the basics of puzzle making, you will want to try your hand at creating your own puzzle designs.

Board Puzzles

Board puzzles—also called tray puzzles, jigsaw puzzles and insert puzzles—are all similar in that they lay flat, and when all of the pieces are assembled, the end result is a picture, shape or design.

The full-size board puzzle designs offered in this chapter are all suitable for toddler age children and can easily be modified to make them more difficult or easier to assemble. To make them easier, eliminate some of the cut lines so the pieces are larger and fewer in number. For more difficulty, add more cut lines so there will be more pieces. However, don't make the pieces smaller if the puzzle is to be used for children three years of age or younger. Small parts present a choking hazard to children.

Generally speaking, board puzzles are considered of average difficulty (for a ten-year-old) if the pieces are about 1″ square. For seven-year-old children, average difficulty comes from pieces about 1½″ square. Toddlers should find puzzle pieces around 3″ square challenging.

Board puzzles are made from two layers of material, most commonly a better quality ¼″-thick hardwood veneer plywood top layer and a ¼″-thick hardboard or similar backing layer. Hardboard, often called Masonite, is available in two types: standard and tempered. As a rule, tempered is more waterproof and stronger than standard. If you want to cut costs, consider using lauan, fir or other suitable ¼″-thick sheet materials for the backing.

Because board puzzles are made from ¼″-thick plywood, they lend themselves well to mass production. Almost any scroll saw can cut several layers of ¼″-thick plywood at the same time when stack sawing techniques are used. Work slowly and carefully, as any mistakes will be duplicated in all layers.

Making Board Puzzles: Step by Step

1 Begin by transferring the pattern to the top plywood piece. Use carbon paper to trace the pattern directly to the stock. You can also photocopy the pattern and use spray adhesive to secure the photocopy to the stock. Be sure the pattern is centered on the plywood. One thing you might want to do before transferring the pattern is to sand the surface. This will reduce the amount of sanding that will be required after the pieces have been cut.

2 Next, a pilot hole must be drilled so the scroll saw blade can be threaded through to make the cuts. As a rule, use the smallest drill bit possible to make a pilot hole. Whenever possible, drill the pilot hole at the junction of two or more lines—here the pilot hole will be less obvious in the finished puzzle than if simply drilled on a cut line.

3 Thread a reverse-tooth scroll saw blade through the pilot hole; then install the top end of the blade into the blade holder. Begin cutting out the pattern. After all the cuts have been made, turn off the saw, disconnect the top end of the blade, and remove the outer frame.

4 Next, sand each puzzle piece until smooth. Additionally, all edges should be rounded slightly to make the pieces easy to handle by small hands. Round off (slightly) any sharp corners or edges—these do not take a finish well and tend to break if the pieces are forced into place.

5 Attach the frame to the backing board. The best way to do this is with woodworking glue. First, make certain that the backing board is exactly the same size as the frame. Then, apply a bead of woodworking glue to the mating surfaces of both the frame and the backing board. Press the pieces together making sure

Always sand the puzzle surface before laying out the pattern. This will result in a better puzzle.

Choose a location for a pilot hole that will not be apparent in the finished puzzle.

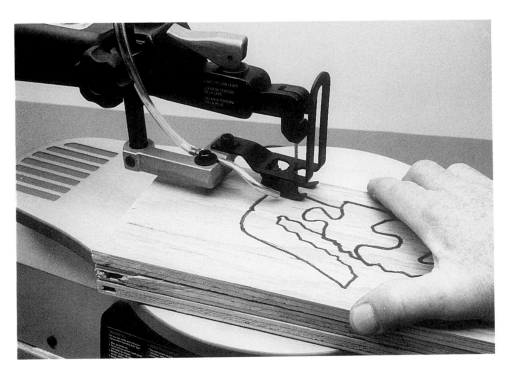

When making more than one copy of a puzzle, consider stack sawing as a quick method of getting the job done.

that all edges are even.

Now the frame and the backing board must be clamped until the glue sets. Use several C-clamps or simply add about 10 pounds of weight to the boards (a few one-gallon paint cans or a stack of books will do the job nicely). If using weights, place a scrap sheet of plywood over both the puzzle frame and the backing board. Let this "sandwich" sit overnight so the glue has sufficient time to set up.

Use a damp cloth to wipe off any excess glue that oozes from between the two boards. If, after the glue has set, you discover any hardened glue drops, carefully remove them with a sharp wood chisel. Hardened glue drops inside the frame will prevent the puzzle from being assembled properly.

6 Now the board puzzle is ready for painting and finishing. Some color suggestions are included with each pattern, but feel free to substitute any colors that appeal to you. After the paint has dried, add the eye, ear, nose and any other details with a waterproof felt-tip pen or India ink and pen. This will prevent bleeding of the ink, as unfinished wood tends to wick ink, which results in less than crisp details. A clear finish

Use enough clamps and clamping aids to ensure a good bond.

This is an effective way of holding the pieces together while the glue sets.

Some softwoods will "bleed" if not sealed before adding detail.

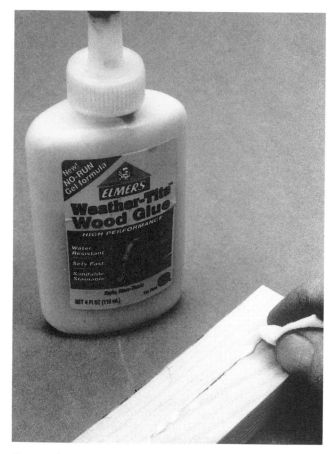

Use a damp rag to remove any excess glue before it dries.

is next. Polyurethane can be applied with a brush, or you can use a spray finish like Krylon. Apply the finish to the entire puzzle.

One caution worth mentioning is that some paints and finishes may be toxic until cured. Since most puzzles will be used by children, make certain that the finishes you will be applying are safe for use around small children. If you are in doubt, check with the manufacturer—often there will be a toll-free telephone number on the packaging so you can call the manufacturer for information about their product.

Five Board Puzzle Patterns
Duck Board Puzzle

Duck board puzzle pattern.

Materials Required

Top—¼″ birch veneer plywood 7 × 10″

Backer board—¼″ tempered hardboard 7 × 10″

Woodworking glue

Paint and clear finish

Time required: 2 hours

Suggested Colors: yellow for the mother duck, white for the duckling and frame.

Enlarge pattern 150%

Dinosaur Board Puzzle

Dinosaur board puzzle pattern.

Materials Required

Top—¼″ birch veneer plywood 7 × 10″

Backing board—¼″ tempered hardboard 7 × 10″

Woodworking glue

Paint and clear finish

Time required: 2 hours

Suggested Colors: dark green for the adult dinosaur, light green or yellow for the baby dinosaur, white for the frame.

Enlarge pattern 150%

This dinosaur board puzzle is sure to please any child.

Elephant Board Puzzle

Elephant board puzzle pattern.

Materials Required

Top—¼″ birch veneer plywood 8 × 10″

Backing board—¼″ tempered hardboard 8 × 10″

Woodworking glue

Paint and clear finish

Time required: 2 hours

Suggested Colors: gray for the elephant and white for the frame.

Add tusks and toe nails if you like.

Enlarge pattern 150%

This elephant board puzzle is not too difficult for a toddler.

Pig Board Puzzle

Pig board puzzle pattern.

Materials Required

Top—¼″ birch veneer plywood 7 × 10″

Backing board—¼″ tempered hardboard 7 × 10″

Woodworking glue

Paint and clear finish

Time Required: 2 hours

Suggested Colors: pink for the pig and white for the frame. Or, you can use black paint for the front half of the pig and white paint for the back half.

Enlarge pattern 150%

Horse Board Puzzle

Horse board puzzle pattern.

Materials Required

Top—¼″ birch veneer plywood 9 × 10″

Backing board—¼″ tempered hardboard 9 × 10″

Woodworking glue

Paint and clear finish

Time required: 2 hours

Use any suitable color to paint the horse. Add spots if you like. Or, paint the horse to look like a palomino (a golden color with a white mane and tail). Paint the frame white. Also, consider adding hoof and mane details.

Enlarge pattern 150%

Stand-Alone Puzzles

Stand-alone puzzles are unique in that when assembled they resemble an animal or shape that can be picked up and moved easily. These types of puzzles are popular with small children and adults because of the cleverness of the design.

There are patterns for five stand-alone projects in this chapter, three animal shapes (elephant, teddy bear and alligator) and two brainteasers. These stand up puzzles won't require much stock, so check your scrap bin before buying any material; it might just yield all the stock you'll need.

Also, you won't need a lot of time to make stand-up puzzles. Most of these projects can be completed in an hour or two. Anyone with a busy schedule will find that a real plus.

If the puzzle is to be used by children three years of age or younger, don't cut the parts smaller than shown in the full-size patterns. Small parts can present a choking hazard to young children.

Choosing Stock

As a rule, stand-alone puzzles are cut from solid wood or plywood that is at least ¾″ thick. This is a minimum thickness required for the puzzle to stand properly and stay together. Generally, solid wood is suitable for most stand-alone puzzles unless certain parts have fragile short-grain areas. In such cases, plywood may be a better choice.

Plywood
If you decide to use plywood for stand-alone puzzles, use only quality cabinet grades. It should have

This is a fun stand-alone puzzle for children.

2×4 lumber can be edge-joined with glue and clamps to give you wider stock for stand-alone puzzles.

two good sides—commonly referred to as A/A grade. Keep in mind that you can laminate two or more layers of ½″-thick plywood to make thicker plywood. When the edges of the puzzle are well sanded, the project will have an interesting look.

Solid Wood

Solid wood is used for most stand-alone puzzles. There is a wide selection of solid wood from which to choose. Standard dimensional lumber is probably the most economical. If you need a thick puzzle, consider 2×4 or 2×6 framing lumber, as it results in a puzzle with a 1½″ base. Also, remember that scraps from building sites or your own construction projects are easy to obtain and suitable for many of the stand-alone puzzles in this chapter. Standard construction lumber is pine, spruce and fir.

When selecting scraps of dimensional lumber, avoid pieces that have knots, checks, twists or irregular grain patterns. These defects, while not crucial for framing lumber, could affect how a puzzle looks or goes together. Choose pieces that are straight grained and free of defects.

Often dimensional lumber will have slightly rounded edges, and these should be planed before laying out the puzzle pattern. This can be done by hand with a plane or on a planing machine. The end result should be square edges.

If your puzzle plan calls for wider material, consider gluing two 2×4s edge to edge. Use a quality woodworking glue and clamps. This will result in not only the width you require but a combination of grain patterns.

It is also possible to laminate two or more pieces of 1×6 (or wider) lumber to arrive at thicker material for stand-alone puzzles. This can be accomplished quite easily by gluing two or more pieces of 1×6 lumber and clamping until the glue sets up fully. Such a "sandwich" will be much stronger than a single piece of lumber and have little tendency to check, split or warp. Laminated lumber also makes for interesting and unique stand-alone puzzles.

In addition to dimensional lumber (2×4 and 2×6), there are many other choices for stand-alone puzzle material. All of the standard softwood and hardwood varieties are good choices that look attractive when finished with a clear coating so the natural grain pattern and color of the wood shows through clearly. Some of the best choices include soft maple, sugar pine, white pine, poplar and birch. Some of the softer woods—such as willow, butternut, cedar, redwood and pine—are poor choices as they tend to break if the pieces are forced together by a determined small person.

Some hardwoods—oak, hickory, cherry, and most of the exotics—are difficult to work with unless you are using one of the more expensive and precise scroll saws (Excalibur and Hegner to mention two).

Wood Sources

If you have a problem finding suitable softwoods or hardwoods locally, consider one of the many mail-order companies that offer small quantities of lumber for woodworkers. Two that immediately come to mind are: Woodcraft (tel. (800) 225-1153) and The Woodworkers' Store (tel. (800) 279-4441). Call for catalogs.

Choosing A Blade

When cutting out stand-alone puzzles, use the thinnest blade possible to do the job. Unfortunately, you are limited in blade choice as the thicker materials will require a thicker, coarser tooth blade. As a rule, use the thinnest blade possible, but keep in mind the fact that you want a puzzle that will go together and come apart easily.

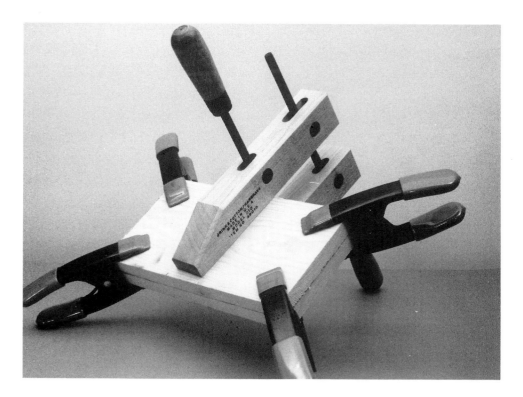

¾"-thick lumber can also be laminated to achieve a suitable thickness for stand-alone puzzles.

Teddy Bear Stand-Alone Puzzle

Teddy Bear stand-alone puzzle pattern.

Materials Required

2 × 6 dimensional lumber or 8 × 8″ square hardwood, 1½″-thick minimum

Paint or stain and clear coating or linseed oil

Time required: 1 hour

For 2 × 6 enlarge pattern 130%; for 8 × 8, 180%

1 Give both sides of the stock a light sanding to ensure that it is clean and smooth.

2 Transfer the pattern to the stock.

3 Bore a pilot hole for the heart cutout. The best hole location is at the V shape at the top of the heart.

4 Cut along the pattern line, starting at the flat bottom. Cut out along the outline of the bear, then cut the division lines through the body as shown.

5 Disconnect the top end of the blade from the holder. Thread the blade through the pilot hole, then reconnect the blade and cut out the heart shape.

6 Give each of the pieces a thorough sanding, including the edges. Avoid removing too much material or the puzzle parts will have a sloppy fit.

7 Now the bear can be finished. Start by painting all the surfaces. A light to medium brown color would be appropriate, although a puzzle like this will look good painted almost any color. Paint the heart red.

After the paint dries, add the eye, nose and paw detail with a waterproof felt-tip pen or India ink and pen. Adding a light coat of clear finish will complete the project.

As an option, the puzzle can be stained and clear coated or simply coated with a clear finish—polyurethane or linseed oil. Add the pen details between the coats of clear finish.

Alligator Stand-Alone Puzzle

Alligator stand-alone puzzle pattern.

Materials Required

2 × 4 dimensional lumber or 3½ × 9½″ hardwood, 1½″ thick minimum

Paint or stain and clear coating or linseed oil

Time required: 1 hour

Enlarge pattern 150%

1 Lightly sand both sides of the wood to smooth the surface and remove any dirt.

2 Transfer the alligator pattern to the stock.

3 Using the scroll saw, cut out the outer profile of the alligator. Start the cut at the belly. Once the profile is completed, cut the division lines through the body.

4 Sand all the pieces, including their edges. Be careful, however, not to remove too much edge stock. If you do, the puzzle will have a sloppy fit.

5 Paint or stain the alligator green, brown, or any other suitable color. After the paint dries, add the eye detail with a waterproof felt-tip marker or India ink and pen. Apply a coat of clear finish to complete the puzzle.

Pie-Shaped Brainteaser Puzzle

Brain teaser pattern.

Materials Required

Minimum ¾"-thick 6 × 6" hardwood, softwood or combination of woods

Stain and/or clear finish

Time required: 1 hour

Enlarge pattern 150%

This pie-shaped puzzle is made from ¾"-thick hardwood cut to a 6" diameter. Use thicker hardwood, if you like, but don't use stock that is any thinner. Keep in mind that the pattern is offered as a suggestion, so don't be afraid to make some changes to the shape of the division lines. You can also change the number of parts.

Two factors will influence your success when making this puzzle. First, use the thinnest blade possible. This will make the pieces fit together tightly. Second, make sure that the blade is perpendicular to the table when making the cuts. If it isn't, the pieces will not fit together well. Check the alignment of your blade with a square.

1 Sand both top and bottom surfaces before tracing or attaching the pattern. This will result in a better looking puzzle overall.

2 Cut out the circle first, then cut the division lines.

3 Thoroughly sand all the pieces with sandpaper up to 220-grit. Soften any sharp edges.

4 When using hardwood, this puzzle looks great coated with a clear finish. Apply several light coats of polyurethane or spray with Krylon. As an alternative, stain each of the pieces a different color, then finish with several light coats of clear finish. Linseed oil also looks good. If you like, you can vary the look of this puzzle by cutting each piece from a different type of wood.

Cylinder Brainteaser Puzzle

Brain teaser pattern.

Materials Required

1½"-diameter dowel—8" long—hardwood or softwood

Stain and clear finish

Time required: 1 hour

Enlarge pattern 150%

This is a slightly tricky puzzle for inexperienced scroll sawers but one worth trying. It makes an interesting gift for children as well as adults. The pattern should be used as a guideline, but keep in mind that it is not etched in stone. It can be varied provided you rotate the dowel 15° to 20° after each cut. If you follow this technique, you can cut this type of puzzle from any size cylinder, as long as it is within the capacity of your scroll saw.

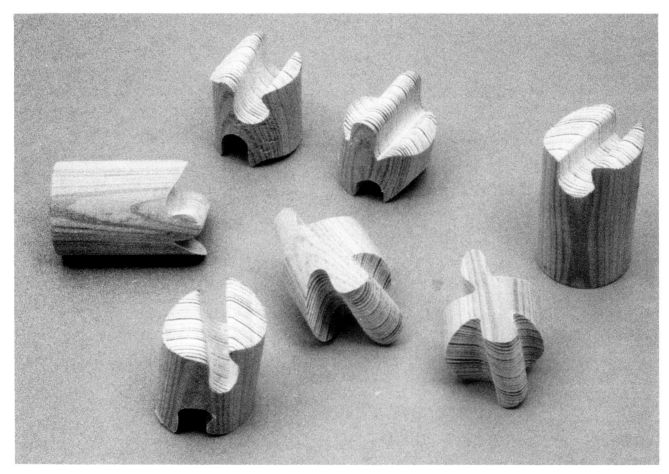

This brainteaser is a fun project that will make most people stop and think about assembly.

1 Sand the entire surface of the dowel using up to 220-grit sandpaper.

2 Transfer the full-size pattern to the dowel. (Remember, the dowel is a bit long so that it will be easier to hold when cutting.) You'll probably find that it's difficult to transfer a flat pattern to a round dowel, but don't worry about getting it exactly as shown, just get it as close as you can.

3 It is difficult to cut any dowel without some type of jig to hold it steady during the cutting work. A quick and easy jig can be made by cutting two lengths of wood into long triangles. Several strips of tape are used to hold the triangles at the required distance. Add tape as needed to keep the dowel firmly supported during all of the cuts.

4 Using the jig, cut along the first division line and remove the first piece. Now, rotate the dowel 15° to 20°, make a second cut, and remove the piece. Continue this procedure until all seven pieces are cut.

5 Trim the excess stock to arrive at the required overall length.

6 Apply a coat of stain followed by two coats of a clear final finish.

Tape two triangle strips to the edges of the cylinder to keep it steady when cutting this brainteaser.

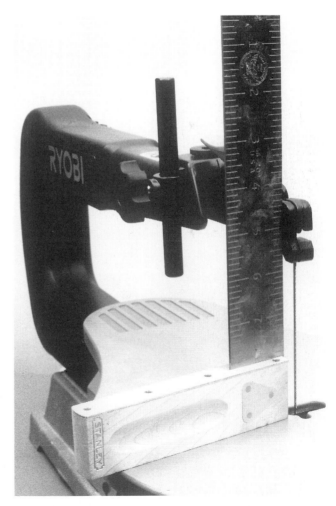

Check the blade of your scroll saw with a square—the blade must be at a 90° angle to the saw table for best results.

CHAPTER SIX

Weather Vanes, Whirligigs, Mobiles and Decoys

Weather vanes are an interesting part of Americana that can easily be made on any scroll saw. While some antique versions of weather vanes—also called wind vanes and weathercocks—were three-dimensional, hand carved or made from metal, many more were simply made from flat stock. Weather vanes actually had two purposes: to help anyone who bothered to look determine the direction of the wind and to provide amusement. Three functional or decorative weather vanes are offered in this chapter.

Weather vanes are functional and are very simple to make on a scroll saw. Once made and painted, a weather vane can be mounted on a roof, barn, silo or post to indicate wind direction. Weather vanes can also be mounted on a brass rod (brass brazing rod works well) and set in a decorative wooden block for use as an indoor decoration. As a rule, if the weather vane will be used outdoors, cut the pattern from exterior grade plywood (½″ works best). For interior use, ¾″-thick softwood (pine or redwood) is a good choice.

Racehorse Weather Vane

Materials Required

Exterior grade plywood ½ × 14 × 24″

⅛″ brass brazing rod 16″ long

Exterior wood primer and suitable paints

Exterior caulk

For Interior Use:

¾ × 14 × 24″ softwood (pine or redwood)

2 × 4 × 10″ redwood for base plate

⅛″ brass brazing rod 10″ long

Time required: 3 hours

One square = 1″

1 Begin by enlaring the pattern on a copier. Tape the sections of the pattern together so you have a full pattern.

2 Next, transfer the pattern to the face of the plywood using carbon paper and a rounded pencil, or use spray adhesive (on the back of the pattern) and attach the pattern directly to the plywood.

3 Drill a pilot hole below the jockey's arm and cut this section out first. Next, cut out the remainder of the pattern using a reverse-tooth scroll saw blade to

Racehorse Weather Vane pattern.

minimize tear-out on the back of the plywood. Since the adhesives used to make plywood are abrasive, you may find it necessary to replace the blade halfway through the cutting process.

4 Sand all surfaces smooth by hand or with a power sander. Next, drill a ⅛″-diameter hole (indicated by the dashed line) about 2″ deep. It is important that this hole be centered and straight, as the brass rod will be inserted here.

5 Begin finishing by applying a coat of exterior primer. After this dries, paint the horse body. Once dry, paint the tail, mane, jockey and saddle. Paint eye and hoof detail if desired. After all paints have dried, it is time to install this weather vane in a suitable location.

6 To mount, drill a ⅛″ hole about 4″ deep— possible locations include the gable end of a roof or on a post. Cut enough brass rod to insert into the hole, extend about 8″ and to fit 2″ into the bottom of the weather vane (about 14″ total). Fill the hole in the mounting location with caulking before inserting the brass rod. Next, install the brass rod and weather vane. Do not caulk the hole in the weather vane—this would prevent it from swinging freely in the wind.

7 If your weather vane will be used indoors, it can be mounted on a wooden block or attached to an interior wall. Begin by drilling a ⅛″-diameter hole (1″ deep) in the center of the redwood block. To mount, cut enough brass rod to fit into the block, extend about 8″, and fit into the bottom of the weather vane (about 11″ total). Insert the rod into the hole in the block, tap with a hammer to stabilize and install the weather vane on top of the rod.

Two variations for interior use worth mentioning are to stain the horse body or to simply finish with a clear coating. This project will look best if the jockey's silks and saddle are painted bright colors, however.

Pig Weather Vane

Materials Required

Exterior grade plywood ½ × 12 × 22"

⅛" brass brazing rod 12" long

Waterproof woodworking glue

#4 finish nails (4)

Exterior wood primer (white) and black body paint

Exterior caulk

For Interior Use:

¾ × 12 × 22" softwood (pine or redwood)

2 × 4 × 6" for base plate

Woodworking glue

#4 finish nails (4)

⅛" brass brazing rod 10" long

Time required: 2 hours

---

1 Begin by enlarging the pattern on a copier—make two copies, as two ears are required for this project. Next, transfer the pattern (including two ears) to the face of the plywood using carbon paper and a rounded pencil, or use spray adhesive (on the back of the pattern) and attach the pattern directly to the plywood.

2 Cut out the pattern using a reverse-tooth scroll saw blade to minimize tear-out on the back of the plywood. Since the adhesives used to make plywood are abrasive, you may find it necessary to replace the blade halfway through the cutting process. Next, cut out the two ears.

3 Sand the body and both ears smooth by hand or with a power sander. Next, drill a ⅛"-diameter hole (indicated by the dashed line) about 2" deep. It is important that this hole be centered and straight, as the brass rod will be inserted here. Attach the ears (facing forward and slightly down) to both sides of the head, using waterproof woodworking glue and #4 finish nails.

4 Begin finishing by applying a coat of exterior primer. After this dries, paint the pig body—note that the rear half and the head are painted black, but the shoulders are left white. Paint eye detail if desired. After all paints have dried, it is time to install this weather vane in a suitable location.

5 To mount, drill a ⅛" hole about 4" deep—possible locations include the gable end of a roof or barn, or on a post. Cut enough brass rod to insert into the hole, extend about 6" and fit 2" into the bottom of the weather vane (about 12" total). Fill the hole in the mounting location with caulking before inserting the brass rod. Next, install the brass rod and weather vane. Do not caulk the hole in the weather vane, as this would prevent it it from swinging freely in the wind.

If your weather vane will be used indoors, it can be mounted on a wooden block or attached to an interior wall. Begin by drilling a ⅛"-diameter hole (1" deep) in the center of the redwood block. To mount, cut enough brass rod to fit into the block, extend about 6", and fit into the bottom of the weather vane (about 9" total). Insert the rod into the hole in the block, tap with a hammer to stabilize, and install the weather vane on top of the rod.

Two variations for interior use worth mentioning are to stain the pig body or to simply finish with a clear coating.

Pig Weather Vane Pattern

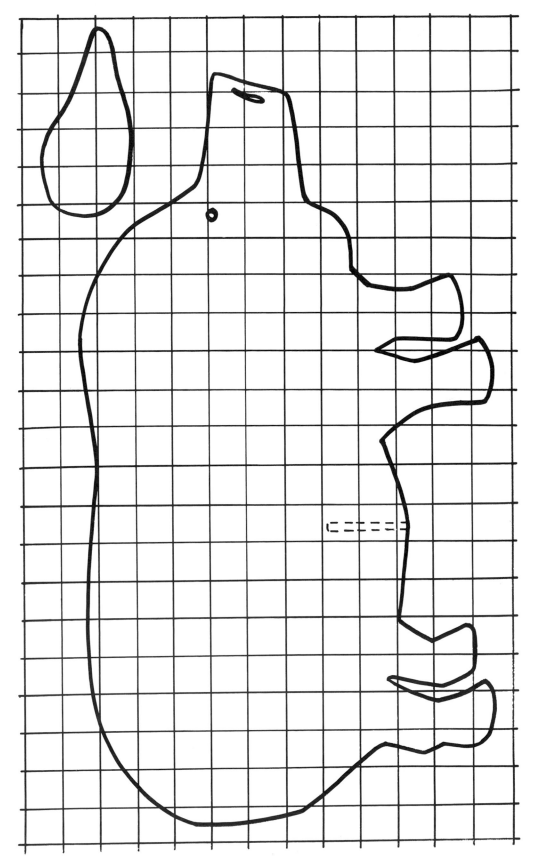

Goose Weather Vane

Materials Required

Exterior grade plywood ½ × 19 × 25"

⅛" brass brazing rod 10" long

Exterior wood primer (white) and black body paint

Exterior caulk

For Interior Use:

¾ × 19 × 25" interior plywood

2 × 4 × 12" for base plate

⅛" brass brazing rod 9" long

Time required: 2 hours

One square = 1"

---

1 Begin by copying the pattern on a copy machine—make several copies until this pattern is enlarged to a suitable size. As an aid, each square is one inch.

2 Next, transfer the pattern to the face of the plywood using carbon paper and a rounded pencil, or use spray adhesive (on the back of the pattern) and attach the pattern directly to the plywood.

3 Cut out the pattern using a reverse-tooth scroll saw blade to minimize tear-out on the back of the plywood. Since the adhesives used to make plywood are abrasive, you may find it necessary to replace the blade halfway through the cutting process.

4 Sand the body by hand or with a power sander.

5 Next, drill a ⅛"-diameter hole (indicated by the dashed line) about 3½" deep. It is important that this hole be centered and straight, as the brass rod will be inserted here.

6 Begin finishing by applying a coat of exterior primer. After this dries, paint the body—note that the entire goose is black except for a slash of white behind the jaw and below the eye. Paint eye detail (yellow) if desired. After paint has dried, it is time to install this weather vane in a suitable location.

7 To mount, drill a ⅛" hole about 4" deep— possible locations include the gable end of a roof or barn or on a post. Cut enough brass rod to insert into the hole, extend about 6", and fit 3½" into the bottom of the weather vane (about 13½" total). Fill the hole in the mounting location with caulking before inserting the brass rod. Next, install the brass rod and weather vane. Do not caulk the hole in the weather vane, as this would prevent it from swinging freely in the wind.

If your weather vane will be used indoors, it can be mounted on a wooden block or attached to an interior wall. Begin by drilling a ⅛"-diameter hole (1" deep) in the center of the redwood block. To mount, cut enough brass rod to fit into the block, extend about 6", and fit into the bottom of the weather vane (about 10½" total). Insert the rod into the hole in the block, tap with a hammer to stabilize, and install the weather vane on top of the rod.

Goose Weather Vane Pattern

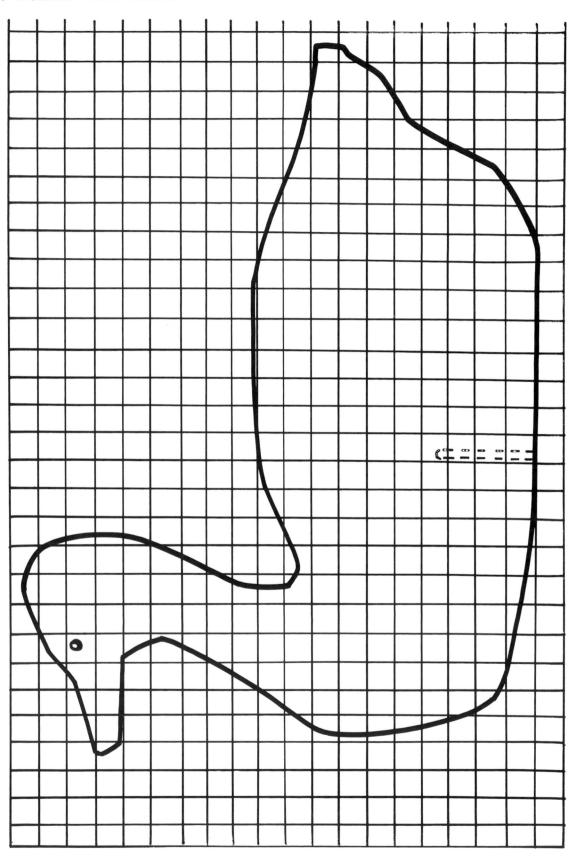

Whirligigs

No doubt whirligigs—often called wind toys—are an extension of simple weather vanes. The whirligig has evolved as a truly American folk art, and building one is not only a fun exercise in scroll sawing but also an exercise in design and physics. Whirligigs are not only whimsical, they are practical as well. In addition to indicating wind direction, a whirligig will also tell wind velocity—the stronger the wind force, the faster the whirligig whirls. You will learn how to make two whirligigs in this chapter.

Flying Duck

Materials Required

Body—$\frac{1}{2} \times 10 \times 25''$ exterior plywood

Wings (4)—$\frac{1}{8} \times 4 \times 12''$ exterior plywood

Wing blocks (2)—$1\frac{3}{8} \times 1\frac{3}{8} \times 3\frac{5}{8}''$ pine

Wing extensions (2)—$\frac{1}{2} \times 3 \times 11''$

$\frac{1}{4}''$ steel rod 8" long

(2) 2" lag bolts

(4) galvanized washers

Waterproof woodworking glue

Exterior wood primer and suitable exterior paint colors

Time Required: 6 hours

One square = 1"

---

1 Begin by enlarging the pattern on a copy machine. As an aid, each of the squares on the backing grid is one inch. The final pattern will be several pages wide and high. Use tape to construct a full pattern from the pieces.

2 Next, transfer the body pattern to the face of the $\frac{1}{2}''$-thick plywood using carbon paper and a rounded pencil, or use spray adhesive (on the back of the pattern) and attach the pattern directly to the plywood.

3 Cut out the pattern using a reverse-tooth scroll saw blade to minimize tear-out on the back of the plywood. Since the adhesives used to make plywood are abrasive, you may find it necessary to replace the blade halfway through the cutting process. You must also cut out two trapezoid-shaped wing extensions from the $\frac{1}{2}''$ plywood. This is easiest to accomplish by stack cutting. Cut these parts exactly as shown in the diagram.

The four wings are cut from $\frac{1}{8}''$-thick exterior plywood. Now two wing blocks must be cut $3\frac{5}{8}''$ long from square stock that measures $1\frac{3}{8}''$ square. Clear pine is suitable for these parts.

4 Next, diagonal slots must be cut on each end of the wing blocks. The slot is $\frac{1}{8}''$ wide and 2" deep. The diagonals must be cut in opposite directions to give the propeller the necessary twist. Also, you will need to bore a $\frac{1}{4}''$ hole in the center to accept a $\frac{3}{16}'' \times 2''$-long lag screw.

5 Drill a $\frac{1}{8}''$ hole $\frac{3}{4}''$ deep into the top edge of both wing extensions. These holes will serve as mounting holes for the wing assemblies. Drill a $\frac{1}{4}''$ hole about $2\frac{1}{2}''$ deep through the edge of the belly area. This will serve as a mounting hole for the steel rod. The angle for this hole is approximately 80°.

6 Sand all parts by hand or use a power sander. All surfaces must be smooth and ready for assembly and finish.

7 Attach the wings to the wing blocks using waterproof woodworking glue.

8 Attach one trapezoid part to each side of the duck's body as indicated in the diagram— rectangular area running about midway along the body. Use waterproof woodworking glue and #4 finish nails for this. Toenail these parts to the body.

9 Before further assembly, all parts should be finished. Begin by coating all surfaces with exterior primer. Then paint the body, head and wings. One suggestion is to make a mallard drake—green head, brown body and wings, and black wing tips with a white stripe. Add eye detail (yellow).

10 After all parts are dry, assemble this duck whirligig. Attach the wing blocks to the wing extensions on the body. Use washers between the wing blocks and wing extensions and under the lag bolt heads. Turn the screws far enough to hold the wing blocks in place but not so far as to restrict wing movement.

11 Now the duck whirligig can be mounted in a suitable location. Probably the best location is a post set in the ground or on a corner post of an existing fence. Drill a ¼″ hole 4″ deep in the top center of the post. Fill the hole with caulking and insert the steel rod. Give a few taps to the top of the rod to seat it well in the top of the post. Last, slip the duck whirligig over the steel rod and wait for the wind to blow.

Flying Duck Pattern

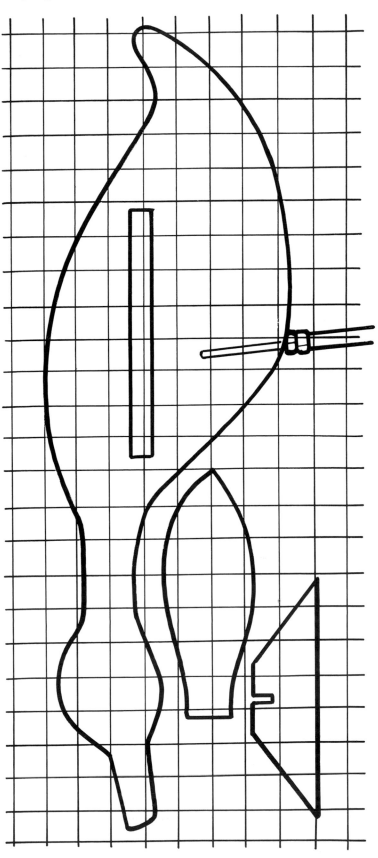

Windmill Whirligig

Materials Required

(2) ¾ × 4¼ × 6¼″ pine or redwood—windmill tower

(3) ¾ × 1¾ × 3½″—roof

(1) 2 × 4 × 7″—base

(2) ¾ × ¾ × 5½″—blades

(1) ¾ × 3 × 3½″—tail vane

(1) ³⁄₁₆″ wooden dowel 3″ long

(1) Flathead wood screw

#8 finish nails

Waterproof woodworking glue

Exterior primer and exterior paints (black, red and white)

Time required: 6 hours

Full-size patterns on pages 108 and 109.

1 Begin by copying the patterns given (they are actual size) on a copier. Next, trace the tower pattern twice, blade pattern twice, roof pattern four times and tail vane once.

2 To save time and cutting effort, stack cut where possible—the cutting capacity of your scroll saw must be at least 1½″ to cut two layers.

3 Cut the 2 × 4 lumber to length for the base.

4 Using waterproof woodworking glue and clamps, glue the two tower pieces together. Make certain that all edges are even before clamping.

5 Next, glue and clamp the four roof sections together, carefully aligning all edges before clamping tightly. Wipe off any excess glue with a damp cloth before it hardens. While you are waiting for the glue to set up, you can turn your attention to the blades of the windmill.

6 The blades for this windmill require the most work and are the most difficult parts to cut. Begin by drawing a pencil line from the top of one end corner to the bottom of the opposite end corner. Duplicate this line on the second blade. When complete, both blades should have identical lines running at an angle from one corner to the other.

7 Next, lay one blade on top of the other so they form a right angle, with the length of each blade equal to the others. Mark pencil lines on both blades where they cross. Pencil in a ⅛″ deep area where the blades should be cut out in order to fit together.

8 Next, the blades must be shaped by cutting. Your intention is to remove equal amounts of material on both sides of a blade until the remaining thickness is about ³⁄₁₆″. Repeat this cutting on the other end of the blade in hand. After one complete blade has been cut in this manner, repeat the process on the other blade. Then make the cutout so the blades can be fit together.

Draw pencil lines from one corner to the opposite corner to lay out windmill blade.

9 Sand all windmill parts smooth by hand or with a power sander. Round off and generally smooth all edges by hand sanding. Sand the blades smooth at this time as well.

10 Mark and then drill a 3/32" hole in the center face of the windmill roof. Next, mark and drill a 7/32" hole in the center of the underside of the roof. Also mark and drill a 1/16 hole in the center top of the tower. Although these holes will hold the same rod, only the top section should be free to move—in effect, the bottom hole (in the top of the windmill body) securely holds the pivot rod for the roof.

11 Drill a 3/16" hole in the center of the back face of the roof. Drill another 3/16" hole in the edge of the tail vane. Fit the two blades together by their corresponding slot cuts and drill a 3/32" hole in the center where the blades cross.

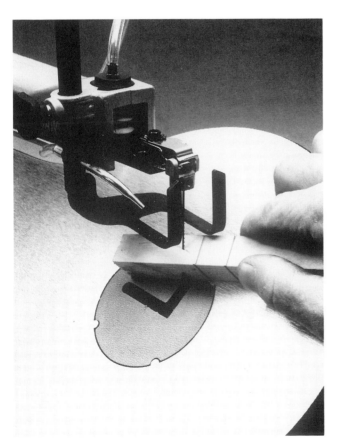

Cut each blade on a scroll saw.

12 It is easier to finish all parts before final assembly. Begin by lightly sanding all parts. Next, prime all surfaces with a light coat of exterior primer. Once the primer dries, paint the tower, roof face and blades white. Paint the base black, and paint a small window part way up the tower and a small door at the bottom center. Paint the roof, tail vane and blade tips red. Once all parts have dried, assemble the windmill.

13 Attach the tower to the center of the 2 × 4 base. Use waterproof woodworking glue and #8 finish nails (driven from below). Glue the 3"-long wooden dowel to the tail vane, and glue this assembly to the center rear of the roof.

14 Install the blades by driving the flathead screw through the front and into the face hole in the roof.

15 Last, cut the head off a #8 finish nail and place this into the hole in the top of the windmill, pointed side up. Tap with a hammer to secure. Next, place the roof section (with hole in the bottom center) on top of this nail. The roof should rotate freely. The blades of the windmill should also rotate easily. If they do not, back the wood screw off slightly until the blades turn freely. Now the windmill is ready for setting out in a suitable location in the garden.

Windmill Whirligig Pattern

Blade

Tail Vane

Windmill Whirligig Pattern

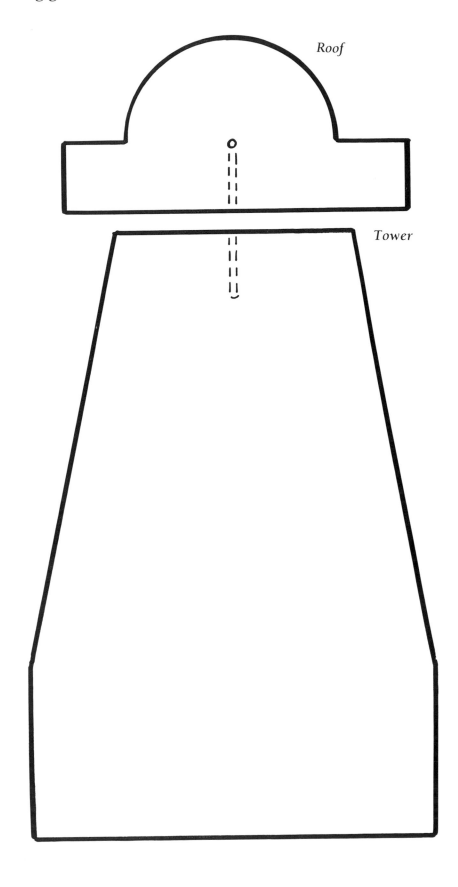

Roof

Tower

Mobiles

Mobiles are another popular craft and art form that can easily be made on your scroll saw. Generally speaking, mobiles are not static but move with the slightest air current and constantly change their form. Mobiles can be hung indoors or out and can be made from a wide range of materials; we will only cover three wooden versions in this chapter.

Animal Mobile

Materials Required

⅜″ lumber—scraps at least 3″ square for each animal

³⁄₁₆″ steel or brass welding rod 30″ long, or steel coat hanger wire

Monofilament fishing line

4 (minimum) ¼″ brass screw eyes

Stain and clear finish, or brightly colored paints

Waterproof felt-tip pen or India ink and pen

Time required: 3 hours

Full-size patterns on pages 112 and 113

1 Begin by copying the patterns for the small animals given in this section. These are full-size patterns. The basic design for this mobile calls for four animals but can be expanded easily by adding more fishing line and straight wires. For this basic mobile, choose four miniature animals that you or your favorite small person might like.

2 Transfer the four patterns to the face of the lumber using carbon paper and a round-tipped pencil, or use spray adhesive (on the back of the patterns) and attach the patterns directly to the lumber.

3 Cut out the patterns using a suitable scroll saw blade.

4 After cutting, sand all surfaces and round all edges slightly. A folded sheet of sandpaper works well for sanding in hard to reach areas, such as around legs, tails and ears.

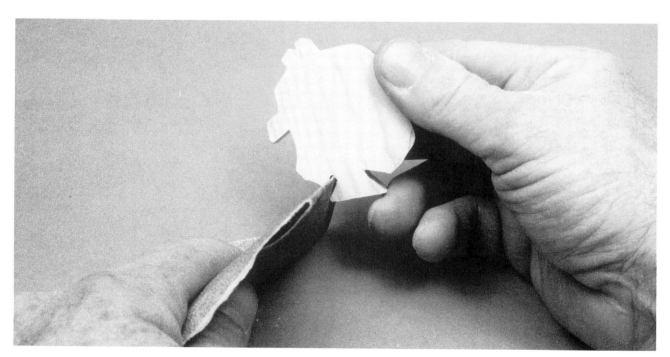

Sand difficult areas with a piece of folded sandpaper.

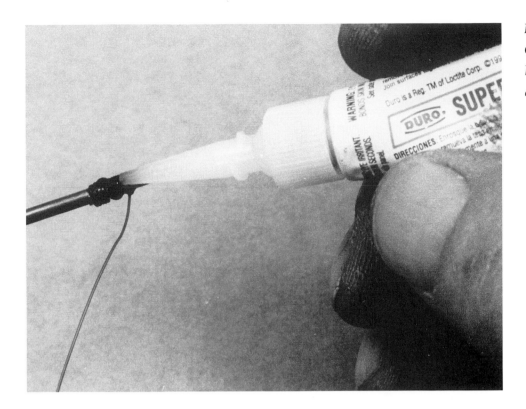

Put a drop of Super Glue on each knot to keep it from coming undone.

5 Finish off each animal either by staining and clear coating or by painting suitable colors. Add eye and other details after the first coat of clear finish or paint. Finish each piece with a clear coat.

6 Now the basic mobile frame can be constructed. You must first cut the steel or brass rod as follows: (1) 16″ and (2) 8″ pieces.

7 Next, tie a length of monofilament fishing line to the center of the long rod. The length of this line should be about 3′ if this mobile will be hung from a standard 8′-high ceiling.

8 Next, tie a 6″ piece of monofilament line to one end of the long rod. Tie the other end to the center of one of the shorter rods. Repeat this for the other short rod, but use a 10″ length of fishing line. Tie lengths of monofilament line to both ends of each of the short rods. Tie one 4″ length to one end and a 6″ length to the other end. Repeat for the other short rod.

9 Screw a brass screw eye into the top center of each animal. This is an important balance point, as each animal will be suspended from this point. Tie the loose end of each line (at the ends of both short rods) to an animal. Add a drop of Super Glue adhesive to each knot to prevent unraveling. The last step is to hang this mobile in a suitable location.

Animal Mobile Pattern A

Animal Mobile Pattern B

Flying Fish Mobile

Materials Required

⅜″ stock—scraps at least 3″ square for each fish

³⁄₁₆″ steel or brass welding rod 30″ long, or wire coat hanger

Monofilament fishing line

4 (minimum) ¼″ brass screw eyes

Stain and clear finish or brightly colored paints

Waterproof felt-tip pen or India ink and pen

Time required: 3 hours

1 Begin by photocopying the full-size fish patterns. The basic mobile design requires four fish, but you can use more simply by adding extra rods and fishing line.

2 Transfer the fish patterns to your stock. Use carbon paper to trace the profiles onto the wood. Or, apply a coat of spray adhesive to the back of the photocopied patterns and mount them directly to the stock.

3 Using a suitable scroll saw blade, carefully cut out each of the fish patterns.

4 Give each cutout a thorough sanding, finishing with 220-grit. Take particular care to round and smooth the edges. Use the folded edge of a piece of sandpaper to get into tight corners.

5 Apply the final finish to the cutouts. You have several choices. If you want the natural color of the wood to show, use one of the clear finishes like shellac, lacquer, polyurethane, or even a clear penerating oil. Or, you can stain the wood before adding one of the clear finishes. Another option is to paint them with bright enamel paints. Allow the finish to dry completely before going on to the next step.

6 Screw a brass screw eye into the top edge of each fish. Try to locate the eye near the center, so the cutout will be balanced when hung from the fishing line.

7 The mobile can now be assembled. You'll need three lengths of ³⁄₁₆″-diameter steel or brass welding rod—two of them measuring 8″ long and the other measuring 16″ long. Also needed are several feet of monofilament fishing line.

8 Tie a length of monofilament fishing line to the middle of the 16″ rod. The entire mobile will be suspended from this line, so you'll want it long enough to permit the mobile to be hung at a suitable height.

9 Tie a 6″ line to one end of the 16″ rod. Then, at the opposite end of the rod, tie a 10″ long line.

10 Tie the end of the 6″-long line to the middle of one of the 8″ rods. Tie the end of the 10″-long line to the middle of the other 8″ rod.

11 Tie a 4″-long line to one end of each 8″ rod. Tie a 6″-long line to the opposite end of the two rods.

12 Complete the project by threading the ends of the four lines through the eye hooks. After securing each one with a tight knot, the mobile is ready to be hung.

Screw a brass screw eye into the top of each animal for hanging.

Flying Fish Mobile Pattern

Double-Heart Mobile

Materials Required

¾ × 6 × 7½″ softwood or hardwood

Monofilament fishing line

Super Glue

Stain and clear finish or suitable paint colors

Time required: 2 hours

1 Begin by copying the pattern (on page 107) on a copy machine—the pattern given is full size.

2 Transfer the pattern to the face of the lumber using carbon paper and a rounded pencil, or use spray adhesive (on the back of the pattern) and attach the pattern directly to the work surface.

3 Drill a pilot hole between the two hearts and cut out the smaller heart first. Then cut out the remainder of the pattern, working carefully to follow the pattern lines.

4 Next make a chamfer cut around the edge of the small heart. Begin by drawing a centering pencil line around the edge of the small heart—this will be the cut line. To make this cut, first adjust the table of your scroll saw to 45°, then cut around the heart, following the cut line. After making the cut, sand to remove any sharpness of the edge.

5 Drill two ¹⁄₁₆″-diameter holes for hanging the small heart inside the larger heart outline. Drill one hole through the center of the top of the V on the top of the large heart. Drill another hole in the center of the V shape in the top of the small heart.

6 Sand all parts with 120-grit sandpaper. Smooth all edges and remove any saw marks using sandpaper.

7 The mobile can now be finished. There are several options. Both hearts can be stained and clear coated, or both hearts can be primed and painted suitable colors, or one heart can be stained and the other primed and painted. Finish the hearts as you see fit.

8 After the finish has dried, put a few drops of Super Glue into the hole in the top of the small heart. Insert one end of fishing line into the top of the small heart; the adhesive should hold the fishing line in place. Next, tie a knot in the fishing line as shown in the pattern, then thread it through the large heart. The location of this knot should make the small heart hang midway inside the larger heart. The remaining free end of the line is for hanging from a ceiling hook or other suitable location. Clip off the excess line once the double-heart mobile has been hung to your satisfaction.

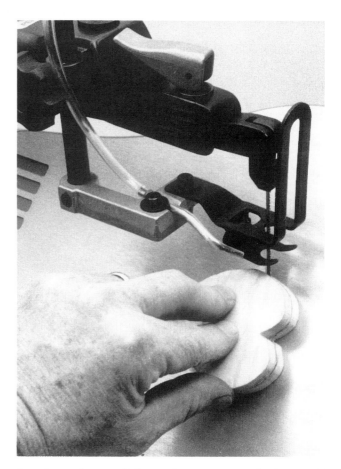

Bevel cut the small heart by cutting with the scroll saw table angled to 45°.

Double-Heart Mobile Pattern

Decoys

Duck and goose decoys have been around for centuries—the oldest known decoys date back over 1,000 years. While there are many different decoy designs made from a variety of materials—from papier-mâché to solid cedar—all decoys are used to lure ducks and geese into shotgun range. To this end, the Canada goose silhouette decoys offered in this chapter do the job. They are easy to cut out on a scroll saw, inexpensive to make in quantities, lightweight and effective. Both feeder and sentry goose silhouette decoys are described in this chapter. One sheet of plywood is enough to make a dozen decoys.

Canada Goose Silhouette Decoys

Materials Required

½″ × 19 × 25″ CDX exterior plywood—Sentry

½″ × 10 × 33″ CDX exterior plywood—Feeder

18″ of 10-gauge galvanized wire per decoy (18′ total)

Exterior wood primer

Flat black, white and brown exterior paint

Time required: 6 hours

One square = 1″

Use wire to hold silhouette decoys upright in the field.

1 Begin by enlarging the patterns in sections on a copy machine. As an aid, each square measures one inch. The final patterns will take several pages to complete. Use tape to keep the pattern together. You will find it helpful to make a posterboard template of both the sentry and feeder decoys. This will make laying out the pattern on a sheet of plywood much easier.

2 Trace the patterns on the surface of a sheet of plywood. One 4 × 8′ sheet will yield at least a dozen decoys when laid out properly. As a rule, make two sentry decoys per ten feeder decoys.

3 To make working with a large sheet of plywood easier, you will find it helpful to divide up the plywood into manageable sections. Use a handheld circular saw or saber saw for this initial cutting. Then cut out each decoy on your scroll saw. As an alternative, consider stack cutting where possible. With a handheld circular saw or table saw, crosscut the plywood into five 10″-wide by 4′-long pieces. Trace two feeder decoys on the top sheet and stack cut to make ten feeder decoys. The two sentry decoys can be cut from the remaining piece of plywood, but because of how they must be laid out, they cannot be stack cut.

4 Use a coarse (9 teeth-per-inch) reverse-tooth blade to minimize bottom tear-out. You will find it necessary to change blades often during this cutting project—when cutting starts to go slow or the work begins to smoke, install a new blade.

5 After all goose silhouette decoys have been cut, put a pencil mark about 2″ up from the bottom and centered on the body. Drill a ⅛″ hole through the plywood at this location for all decoys—this hole will receive the wire that will hold each decoy in a standing position in the field.

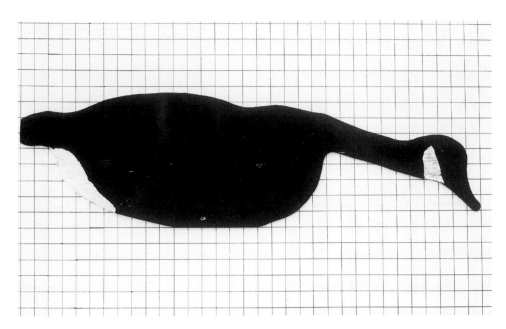

Canada Goose Feeder Silhouette decoy pattern.

Canada Goose Sentry Silhouette decoy pattern.

6 Next, sand all decoys. Remove any rough edges and sand the surfaces smooth. Then apply a coat of exterior primer to all surfaces, including the edges.

7 After the primer dries, paint all silhouettes flat black on both sides, including the edges. Apply flat white exterior paint for cheek slashes and just below the tail. Paint the wings flat brown.

Silhouette goose decoys are light and, because each is only ½" thick, are not bulky, so they are easy to carry.

When set up properly, silhouette goose decoys are just as effective as full-bodied goose decoys.

When setting up these decoys in the field, push an 18" length of 10-gauge galvanized wire through a hole (2" from the bottom and centered) and bend it in half to act as two stabilizing legs. Push these legs down into the soil both to conceal the legs and to add stability in the wind. To add more realism, remove wings from downed birds and staple these to your decoys.

CHAPTER SEVEN

Making Bowls on the Scroll Saw

While bowl making is typically done on a lathe, attractive and functional bowls can also be made on a scroll saw. Unlike lathe work, which turns the workpiece as various carving tools are applied to the surface, a scroll saw is used to cut concentric rings that are glued together to form a bowl. While there are some limitations to making bowls on a scroll saw, you may be surprised at how good such a bowl can look.

Choosing Wood

The two projects in this chapter are constructed from readily available ¾″ lumber. Softwoods such as pine, redwood, fir, basswood, butternut, cypress and poplar are all good choices. Hardwoods such as walnut, maple, birch, hickory, mahogany, oak, cherry, apple and ash are all good choices as well.

There are two requirements for any wood you are considering for a bowl-making project on a scroll saw. The first is that the wood must be free of knots, as these are difficult to cut and can become loose over time. The second requirement is that both faces must be planed flat. Since bowls made on a scroll saw must be glued together, flat surfaces are critical for success.

Plywood can also be used for bowl making, and the effect of the finished bowl can be quite eye

A well-made scroll saw bowl is attractive and useful.

catching. Choose shop or cabinet grade plywood (rather than exterior construction grades) for bowl-making projects as these types are free from surface and internal voids that would prove unacceptable for bowl edges. Plywood contains small amounts of formaldehyde; if you are sensitive to it, avoid using-plywood in your projects.

It is also possible to include different woods, and even plywood, in each bowl. The final bowl

Run lumber through a surface planer to make the surfaces flat and true.

will be much more interesting to look at because of the variety of colors in the layers. Use both light- and dark-colored woods, but arrange the colors before layout and cutting. That way you can achieve the most interesting and pleasing bands of color.

Gluing

All scroll saw bowls are glued together with waterproof woodworking glue. Woodworking glue works well right out of the bottle for most types of hardwoods and softwoods. As a rule, woodworking glue works best for woods that have low density and high porosity. Some woods—such as teak and rosewood—require special attention to remove surface oils before gluing. Wipe difficult woods with acetone and glue up quickly for best results.

Clamping

Clamping is also necessary for scroll saw bowls. You will find it helpful to make a clamping jig to hold the bowl securely as the glue sets. The purpose of the jig is to permit the clamps to exert equal pressure. The size of your jig will be determined by the size of the bowl.

As an example, let's assume you are making a bowl that is approximately 8″ in diameter. To make a suitable clamping jig, you will require two round plywood disks that measure at least 9″ in diameter. Once the bowl rings are cut and glued up, they are stacked on the first disk. After the top piece is glued and positioned on the stack, the second disk is placed on top of the stack, and at least four clamps are positioned to clamp the whole affair until the glue sets fully. When using this clamping jig, it is important to align the rings so that all edges are even. To achieve this, continue to check and align all edges as the clamps are tightened, adjusting the edges as required until all clamps have been sufficiently tightened.

You can also hold the rings in position as the glue sets by simply placing a weight on top of the bowl after all of the rings have been glued and evenly stacked. Use a suitably sized scrap of plywood (at least 1″ wider than the top ring of the bowl) and at least a 10-pound weight.

Choose a variety of different woods for an interesting scroll saw bowl.

Make a clamping jig to glue up a scroll saw bowl.

No matter which method you use, it is important to wipe off any excess glue that may ooze out from the layers. This small act will make finishing the bowl easier when finish sanding. If you discover some hardened glue droplets after the glue has set up, carefully remove them with a sharp chisel.

Sanding the Exterior

After the glue has set, the next step is to sand all surfaces. I have found that a power-sanding tool makes quick work of exterior bowl sanding. A belt sander, stationary belt/disk sander, random orbit sander or palm sander can be used for the exterior. Of course you can also hand sand the exterior, but the process will take much longer. It is important

to keep either the bowl or the sanding tool moving to avoid sanding flat spots on the exterior of the bowl. Use progressively finer grits of abrasive paper (80-, 100-, 150- and 200-grit sizes, for example) until the exterior of the bowl is smooth and uniform. Always sand in a horizontal direction with the grain. Work carefully to avoid flat spots, especially on the bottom and around the top rim.

Sanding the Interior

After the outside of the scroll saw bowl has been sanded to your satisfaction, turn your attention to the inside of the bowl. The inside of a scroll saw bowl poses some problems in that most power-sanding tools will not fit inside the bowl for sanding. In addition, it will not be possible to sand horizontally—with the grain—with most power-sanding tools. The one exception I have found is the Bosch B7000 Corner/Detail Sander.

This Bosch sander (manufactured by S-B Power Tool Company) fits into tight places. The triangle-shaped head orbits at about 13,000 orbits per minute, and the sander's body fits the hand well. Velcro-backed sanding pads in a variety of grit sizes are easy to attach to the sanding head and will help you sand the interior quickly.

Use a power sander on the exterior of the bowl to make the surface smooth and uniform.

Bosch Detail Sander is very handy for sanding the inside of a scroll saw bowl.

Tung oil produces a rich finish.

If you don't have such a sander, the interior must be sanded by hand. Probably the easiest way is to fold a sheet of 80-grit sandpaper in half and start sanding. Then, move up to finer grit sandpaper and continue sanding. Finish off with 200- or finer grit sandpaper. Hand sanding takes time, especially when one or more of the rings have not been glued in perfect alignment.

Finishing

After the bowl has been sanded, you can finish it in a number of ways. The first method is to apply an oil finish. Some of the choices include a linseed oil/beeswax mix (6:1 ratio), walnut oil, tung oil, or one of the many prepared oil mixtures offered in woodworking catalogs. Oil produces a soft, rich finish. As a rule, three coats of oil are applied over a 24-hour period, each application followed by hand rubbing to help the oil penetrate.

The second method of finishing a scroll saw bowl is to apply three coats of a good quality varnish with light sandings between coats. The last coat is sanded with 600-grit sandpaper and is followed with a hand rubbing of mineral oil. Hand rub a finished

Use different woods in each bowl for interesting effects.

bowl about once a month to bring out the richness and natural grain patterns. If you plan to use the bowl with food, use a nontoxic finish like Behlen's Salad Bowl Finish.

The following two projects will produce functional and attractive wooden bowls. The basic dimensions can be changed, but the basic angles and lumber thicknesses must remain the same. It is also possible to change the basic shape of these two bowls. Either can be made square, oval, rectangular or even heart shaped. You can have some fun experimenting with different designs and modifying the patterns, but keep the basic angles and lumber thicknesses constant.

Six-Inch-Wide Bowl

Materials Required

¾ × 6 × 6″ softwood, hardwood, plywood or combination of woods

Waterproof woodworking glue

Oil or varnish finish

Time required: 3 hours

1 Begin by making certain that both top and bottom surfaces are smooth, flat and uniform. Run the lumber through a surface-planing machine if available.

2 Determine and mark the center of the lumber. If the board is square, this can be accomplished by drawing a line from the top right corner to the bottom left corner and another line from the top left corner to the bottom right corner. The point where these two lines cross will be the center of the board.

3 Then, with a drawing compass and ruler, make seven evenly spaced circles starting from the outside edge of the board. The spacing between the rings for this bowl is ⁵⁄₁₆″. Use a ruler to help you adjust the compass and to mark the location of each of the rings.

4 Next, you must drill pilot holes for the scroll saw blade. The cutting angle for this bowl is 22°. Make a jig to guide the drill bit by cutting the end of a piece of scrap lumber to this angle on a power miter saw. If you do not have a power miter saw, use a protractor to determine this angle and cut accordingly. Using this jig, drill six pilot holes, starting at the innermost ring. The outer ring does not require a pilot hole as it can easily be cut from the outside of the board.

5 Adjust your scroll saw table to an angle of 22° and cut the outer ring first. If you are right-handed, keep the work on the left side of the blade as you work. Southpaws make appropriate adjustments. After the outside ring has been cut, disconnect the top

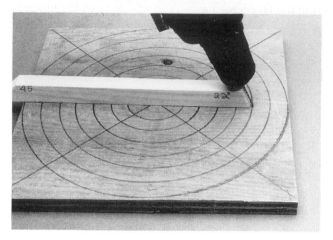

Make a drill guide to help you drill at a 22° angle.

of the blade and thread it through the first pilot hole. Reattach the blade and cut out the next ring. Repeat this process until all rings have been cut out.

While cutting each ring, strive to cut down the center of each cut line. Turn the work into the blade as you go and do not force the lumber into the blade. If you start cutting off the line, get back on track as quickly as possible. Deviations from the cut line will require sanding to achieve a smooth surface on the finished bowl.

6 After all bowl rings have been cut, stack them in order so you can see how the bowl will look. If some edges are cut too deeply or not deeply enough, try repositioning the culprit for better alignment. A little light sanding or twisting a ring left or right just may do the trick. A pencil line run down one side will help to reestablish this alignment as the pieces are glued.

7 Once you are satisfied with the way the bowl stacks, it must be glued and clamped. Begin by applying a thin bead of waterproof woodworking glue to the base and first ring where the pieces will mate. Place the first ring on the base and align with the pencil mark. Repeat this process until all rings have been glued and placed. Then install the clamping jig and clamp the bowl securely. Keep an eye on alignment as you tighten the clamps. Wipe off any excess glue that may ooze out from the layers with a damp cloth. Now let the glue set up fully—usually overnight.

8 After the glue has set, remove the clamps. Look over the bowl and remove any hardened glue drops with a sharp chisel. Work carefully so you don't gouge the surface. Next, sand the exterior and interior of the bowl as described earlier. After all surfaces have been sanded smooth, apply a finish to the bowl.

Eight-Inch-Wide Bowl

Materials Required

¾ × 8 × 8″ softwood, hardwood, plywood or combination of woods

Waterproof woodworking glue

Oil or varnish finish

Time Required: 3 hours

This bowl project is essentially the same as the previous one in technique but, because of the angle of the bevel cut, produces a wider bowl.

1 Using a compass and ruler, make seven evenly spaced circles starting from the outside edge of the board. The spacing between the rings for this bowl is ¾″.

2 Next, you must drill pilot holes for the scroll saw blade. The cutting angle for this bowl is 45°. Make a jig to guide the drill bit as in the previous bowl project.

3 Adjust your scroll saw table to an angle of 45° and cut the outer ring first. After the outside ring has been cut, disconnect the top of the scroll saw blade and thread it through the first pilot hole. Reattach the blade in the top blade holder and cut out the next ring. Repeat this process until all rings have been cut out.

4 After all bowl rings have been cut, stack them in order so you can see how the bowl will look. If some edges are cut too deeply or not deeply enough, try repositioning them for better alignment. A little light sanding or twisting a ring left or right just may do the trick. A pencil line run down one side will help to reestablish this alignment as the pieces are glued.

5 Once you are satisfied with the way the bowl stacks, it must be glued and clamped. Begin by applying a thin bead of waterproof woodworking glue to the base and first ring where the pieces will mate. Place the first ring on the base and align with the pencil mark. Repeat this process until all rings have been glued and placed. Then install the clamping jig and clamp the bowl securely. Keep an eye on alignment as you tighten the clamps. Wipe off any excess glue that may ooze out from the layers with a damp cloth. Now let the glue set up fully—usually overnight.

6 After the glue has set, remove the clamps. Look over the bowl and remove any hardened glue drops with a sharp chisel. Work carefully so you don't gouge the surface. Next, sand the exterior and interior of the bowl as described earlier. After all surfaces have been sanded smooth, apply a finish to the bowl.

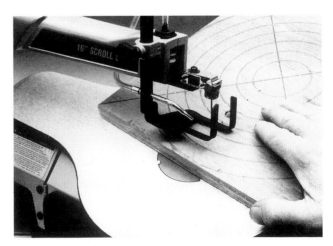

Adjust the scroll saw table to 45° and carefully make the cuts.

CHAPTER EIGHT

Advanced Projects

I n this chapter you will learn a number of techniques that will test your woodworking and
scroll saw skills. You will also see just how versatile
your scroll saw can be. In the first section, you will
be led through the steps of making a dovetailed
box with an inlay top. While this project can be
made using a router, table saw or band saw, all
steps necessary can easily be accomplished using
one tool—your scroll saw. As you become more
proficient at using your scroll saw, you may find
yourself using it for projects that you used other
power tools for in the past.

Other projects in this chapter are exercises in
cutting plastic and metal for Christmas tree ornaments. Another section is a look at marquetry and
is intended to show the basics of this challenging
woodworking art form. The last sections offer a
decorative Victorian arch and decorative Victorian
corner brackets.

Dovetail Box With Inlay Top

As with so many operations in joinery, success in
dovetailing depends on starting with materials that
are square and flat. Check the ends, edges and
surfaces of all materials before starting this project.
Use a square to check these surfaces and a surface
planer or hand plane to make the components true.
Cut all pieces square and to the dimensions given.

Dovetail box with inlay cover.

Materials Required

Ends (2)—⅜ × 3¾ × 6″ sugar pine

Front and back—⅜ × 3¾ × 10″ walnut

Top (1)—⅜ × 6 × 10″ sugar pine

Bottom (1)—⅜ × 5¼ × 9¼″ sugar pine

Top-alignment strip (1)—⅜ × 4⅞ × 8⅛″ sugar pine

Decorative veneer overlay—1/16 × 6 × 10″

Woodworking glue

Contact cement

½″-long wire brads

Oil or clear finish

Time required: 4 hours

1 Begin making this dovetail box by laying out the pins and tails of the joints. The best tool for this is a marking gauge. A pencil, even with a very sharp point, will make a line that is too wide for this part of a dovetail joint. Set the marking gauge 1/32" wider than the thickness of the wood. Now mark the ends on the front, back and two end pieces. This mark will be the depth of all pins and tails.

2 Next, lay out the pins on both the front and back pieces. There are two full pins and two half pins (top and bottom) on each end of these front and back pieces. Mark the waste areas with an *X* to indicate which areas are to be removed. Think about what you are doing and mark both sides and the end-grain area.

3 Adjust the scroll saw table to 15°. Now cut out the left side of all pins. To cut the right side of all pins, you must readjust the scroll saw table to 15° (in the other direction) off-center. If your scroll saw table only adjusts in one direction (as many less expensive models do), you must reverse the blade so that it cuts backward and pulls the work into the blade. Use the thinnest blade possible and cut on the waste side of the line.

4 After all pins have been cut, adjust the scroll saw table back to 90° and cut out the waste areas. When complete, there will be little wedge-shaped pieces next to all pins. Remove these small waste pieces with a sharp knife or chisel.

5 To mark the tails on the ends, clamp the pin piece to the uncut end, align the edges, and mark the tail cuts from the inside. Use a pencil or a sharp awl for this marking. Then, using a T square, extend these marks across the grain. You can use a pencil for these marks. Next, put *X* marks on the waste areas—the parts that will be removed.

6 Cut the tails on the scroll saw. Cut just inside the waste line of the pencil mark. After all cuts have

Use a marking gauge set 1/32" wider than the thickness of the material you are cutting to lay out the pin and tail depth lines.

Lay out the pins and mark the waste areas with an X.

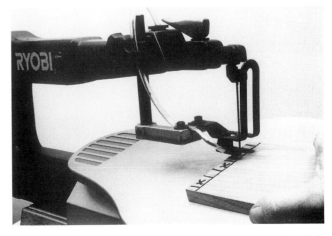

Adjust the scroll saw table to 15° and cut the left side of all pins.

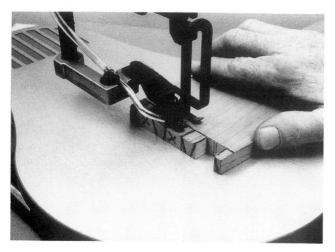

Remove waste area with scroll saw set at 90°.

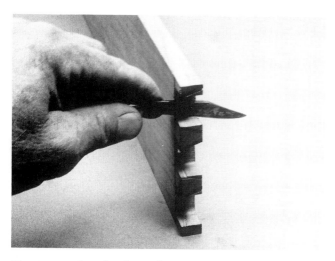

Remove triangle-shaped waste area with a sharp knife.

Clamp pin and tail pieces together evenly and mark the tails.

been made, test fit the joints. Each should be snug but not so tight that it must be forced. Work on one corner at a time, removing material (if required) with a sharp chisel or sandpaper.

7 When you are satisfied with the fit of all joints, sand all surfaces smooth. Then apply a small amount of woodworking glue to all mating surfaces and assemble the box. Next, glue the bottom section in place using woodworking glue as well. Clamp the box to keep all joints together while the glue sets.

Assemble the sides and bottom with woodworking glue and clamp until the glue sets.

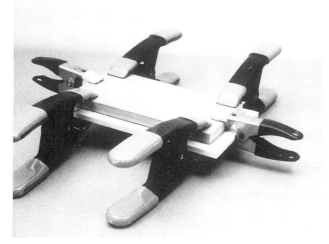

Glue and clamp the top alignment strip to the underside of the cover.

Use contact cement to attach the overlay to the cover.

8 Now assemble the top. First, sand all surfaces smooth; this will make final finishing much easier later. The next step is to install the top-alignment strip on the underside. This strip simply aligns the top to the box and holds it in place. Glue the top-alignment strip in place and clamp until the glue sets up fully.

9 The next step is to install the decorative veneer overlay. There are many different styles available from woodworking companies that specialize in mail order. Some offerings have peel-and-stick backing; others must be glued in place.

Install the decorative veneer overlay. If you are using a peel-and-stick veneer, simply follow directions. If the veneer you are using requires adhesive, probably the best type to use is contact cement. Apply a light coating to the mating surfaces and allow to dry until tacky. Carefully position and attach the veneer. Once in place, use a rolling pin (or veneer roller) to ensure a sound bond.

If the decorative veneer overlay is larger than the top of the box, it must be trimmed. Do this with a sharp knife. Hold the knife blade at about 70° so the edge will be beveled slightly.

Trim any excess veneer with a sharp knife held at a 70° angle to the top surface.

10 To finish this dovetail box, begin by lightly sanding the entire box. Next, apply several coats of an oil finish or three or more coats of a clear finish, such as varnish or polyurethane. Lightly sand between coats. After the final coat has dried, the box is ready for use.

Christmas Tree Ornaments

Christmas tree ornaments make great gifts and, because of the materials they are made from, are unique. While tree ornaments can be made from wood, this section covers ornaments made from both plastic and metal. As a result, I will cover the special techniques required for these materials; then you can use the patterns to make ornaments in your shop.

Cutting Plastic

For our purposes, the word plastic refers to the medium-hard plastics such as acrylics like Plexiglas, Lucite and Acrylite. These materials are available in a variety of thicknesses, colors and surface textures. They should be cut with a coarse scroll saw blade—9 to 12 teeth-per-inch for material thicknesses up to ¼". For thicker sheet plastics, use a scroll saw blade with 6 to 9 teeth-per-inch. You may find a spiral scroll saw blade useful for cutting some of

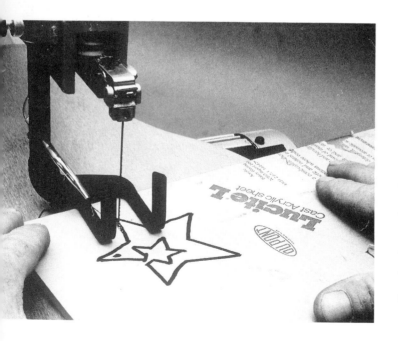

the more intricate snowflakes—experiment.

Most sheet plastics come with a protective coating on both sides. Leave this covering on and trace your pattern over it. The protective covering will help prevent chipping and make the scroll saw blade run a bit cooler. If a protective covering is not present, cover both the top and bottom surfaces with masking tape for the same reasons.

Some experts suggest lubricating the scroll saw blade when cutting plastics. This will help the blade run cooler, and that means a cleaner cut edge. To lubricate a scroll saw blade, make a cut into a block of paraffin or a candle before starting to cut plastic.

Always feed the plastic slowly into the scroll saw blade—never force the cutting, as this will surely cause the blade to heat up. If you begin to smell burning plastic, this is a good indication that you are exerting too much force on the workpiece. A blade speed of about 1000 strokes per minute is good for sheet plastic up to ¼" thick; use a slower speed for thicker material.

Thin sheet plastics (up to ¼" thick) can easily be stack cut. To prevent chipping, leave the protective covering on both sides of all pieces. Use masking tape or double-stick tape to form the stack.

When cutting out the Christmas tree ornament patterns in this section, consider using colored plastic sheet material rather than clear. Some good choices include white, red and green.

Drill pilot holes to cut out interior sections, just as you would if you were making interior cuts in wood. Hang the ornaments by drilling a ¹⁄₁₆" hole at the top of the ornament as required. Consider personalizing Christmas tree ornaments by inscribing a name and year with a handheld engraving tool. This technique works well with both plastic and metal Christmas tree ornaments.

Lubricate the scroll saw blade by making a cut in a block of paraffin or a candle.

Use light oil when cutting metal. This will make the blade run cooler and last longer.

Cutting Metal

All metal cutting on a scroll saw requires the use of a special jewelers' blade. For cutting the projects in this section (brass or aluminum), use a jewelers' blade with 36 teeth-per-inch. Sheet brass usually cuts well at a cutting speed of around 1300 spm. Try this same speed when cutting aluminum, but you may have to decrease the speed if this metal is not cutting smoothly. Aluminum is often a combination of various alloys that can make cutting easy or difficult. For this reason, exact cutting speeds cannot be given for this metal and you must experiment to find the best cutting speed for the particular type of aluminum you are working with.

It makes sense to lubricate a scroll saw blade when cutting metal. Use a light machine oil for this purpose; place a few drops directly on the blade as the cutting progresses. Do this often. Light machine oil has a twofold purpose. It will help the blade run cooler and will result in a smoother cut. Another thing oil will do is help to wash out tiny metal particles (not unlike sawdust when cutting wood) from the cut. Keep a dry rag handy for wiping up excess oil and metal particles as you work.

After cutting, the bottom surface of the cut line will often have burrs. These should be removed with a file. Finish metal Christmas tree ornaments by buffing or polishing, as explained in chapter two.

Materials Required

¼″ Plexiglas or ¹⁄₁₆″ brass or aluminum

Christmas tree ornament hooks

Spray clear finish

Time required: ½ hour each

Snowflake Christmas Tree Ornament Patterns

Marquetry

The art of marquetry has been a creative woodworking form of expression for centuries. Actually, there are many different styles of marquetry from several European countries—most notably France, Italy and England. In Italy, marquetry is still referred to as intarsia. Over the centuries many different materials have been inlaid to produce pictures, floors, walls and fine furniture. In addition to woods of all types, bone, ivory, tortoise shell, mother of pearl, horn, whale bone, marine coral, various metals, plastic, straw and even shagreen (sharkskin) have been used to create amazing marquetry designs.

For our purposes, marquetry is the process of forming inlaid patterns by inserting pieces of wood into a wood veneer that is then laminated to a wooden object. There is a wealth of information about marquetry techniques, materials and designs available—so much so that a single chapter in a book on scroll saws cannot pretend to give more than the basics. To this end, the project we will cover in this section is meant to show you what marquetry is about. Where you go from there is up to you.

Materials Required

4″ square light veneer (any wood)

4″ square dark veneer (any wood)

4″ square ¾″ pine or plywood

Woodworking glue

Oil or clear finish

Time required: 1 hour

Inlaid Plaque

In this exercise we will be cutting a letter from a sheet of veneer. The same letter will also be cut from a different color veneer, then the first letter will be inlaid into the second cutout. Finally, this inlay will be glued to a piece of lumber or plywood to make an initialed plaque. While this may seem like a simple project, there are a number of tricks that will help this project turn out properly.

1 Choose a letter from chapter 3 and enlarge it to about 2″ high. Decide how you would like the grain of the first piece of veneer to run in the finished letter. Next, make the same decision for the second sheet—the one that will hold the inlay.

Many beautiful inlaid patterns can be purchased ready-made to be inserted in your own projects.

The finished project should have no spaces between the letter and background veneer.

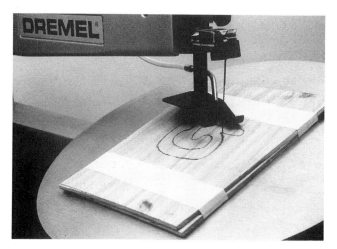

Adjust scroll saw table to 75° and bevel cut the shape. Move the work in a counterclockwise direction.

Glue and clamp the inlay in a "sandwich" of scrap plywood.

2 Trace the pattern onto the surface of the first piece of veneer. Tape the second piece of veneer under the first so both pieces can be cut at the same time with the grain pattern running in the desired direction.

3 Drill a pilot hole with the smallest drill bit that will do the job on the cut line in the least conspicuous spot you can find. Thread a fine-toothed fret blade through the hole.

4 Adjust your scroll saw table so the cut will be beveled. While it is entirely possible to make the cut with the blade set at a 90° angle, the pieces will not fit together as snugly due to the space resulting from the thickness of the scroll saw blade. By bevel cutting, the pieces will fit like they were stamped rather than cut. Adjust the table to about 75° to 80° off-center.

5 Cut out the letter, turning the work in a counterclockwise direction. After cutting, check the fit of the letter into the background. The letter should be slightly larger than the opening but, because of the beveled edges, should fit snugly into place. Tape the letter to the background with masking tape.

6 Now the veneers must be glued to a backing board. Apply a thin coat of woodworking glue to the surface of the backboard and press the veneer assembly over this. Remove any excess glue that may ooze out around the letter or from the edges with a damp rag.

7 Next, with a piece of scrap plywood larger than the backboard make a "sandwich." Clamp the whole affair overnight so that the glue sets up fully.

8 When the clamps are removed, the veneer should be totally bonded to the backboard. Sand the surface smooth. Finish with a few coats of oil or two coats of clear finish.

Victorian Arch

Decorative arches are popular between important rooms in Victorian houses. They are sometimes referred to as "carpenters lace," for obvious reasons. The pattern given in this section is intricate and time-consuming to make, but well worth the effort for an appropriate location. Plywood is a good choice of material, as the finished arch will be much stronger than if made from ¾″ solid stock.

As guidelines: Drill pilot holes and cut inside detail before cutting the profile. Use a reverse-tooth saw blade with 12 teeth-per-inch. You may find cutting some of the smaller details easier if you use a spiral saw blade, but do not use such a blade for the majority of the cutting as it can be difficult to control, especially on long, straight cuts.

If the finished arch will be painted, grain pattern is of little concern. But if the arch will be stained or clear finished, the grain will show. As a rule, the arch will look better if the grain pattern is vertical rather than horizontal. Consider this when laying out the pattern.

The pattern offered in this section will be enough to fill a standard-sized (double pocket door) doorway. The finished arch will contain five pieces. You must enlarge the pattern on a copy machine; each of the five pieces in this arch will consist of several sheets. Tape these together to form a pattern for each piece.

Because you will be cutting ½″ plywood, it is possible to stack cut the pieces. You will require two corner pieces, two second pieces and one center piece. Work carefully and cut the pattern accurately.

Victorian Corner Brackets

Decorative corner brackets are common on the outside of older Victorian homes. While these brackets are commercially available, their cost can be outrageous ($50 and up each!) when you consider it only takes about an hour to make one on a scroll saw.

The decorative corner brackets in this section are made from readily available two-by dimensional lumber. If the brackets will be painted—as they commonly are in restorations—you can also use three or four layers of ¾″ exterior grade plywood that have been glue-laminated together. Glue together after sawing to save wear and tear on saw blades.

Whichever material is used, the cutting is fairly straightforward. Drill pilot holes for making the interior cuts. Make the outline cuts after the interior cuts have been made. Make sure the two flat edges are square so they will fit between the column and roof framing.

When installing these brackets, use a waterproof exterior adhesive and stainless steel or galvanized screws. Countersink and fill all screw holes. Finish with primer and suitable color paint.

Decorative Victorian Arch Pattern

Materials Required

½" thick cabinet or shop grade plywood

Time required: 2 hours per section

Decorative Victorian Corner Brackets

Materials Required

2×8, 2×10 and 2×12 dimensional lumber

Time required: 1 hour per bracket

Intarsia

Intarsia is a type of marquetry that developed in Italy during the Roman Empire. The original technique was called *tarsia certosima* and involved cutting pieces of veneer and then gluing them in cavities that had been carved in solid panels. This technique was used until about the fourteenth century when a new technique—*tarsia geometrica*—was developed in Tuscany. The new technique differed in that the entire surface was decorated with a variety of different veneers rather than inserting them into precut cavities.

During the Renaissance, Italian marqueters developed a process of block marquetry called *tarsia a toppo*, which consisted of making a collage of sticks of wood arranged in stacks. The sticks had different geometric forms so that the end grain produced a unique pattern. The sticks were glued together and then sliced into strips. The end result was patterned bands that could be used for edging and decoration. This technique greatly simplified marquetry in that larger sections could be applied at one time rather than in individual pieces and the work could probably be accomplished by other than a master craftsman.

Around 1620, German marqueters developed another technique—*tarsia a incastro*. This method involved stack cutting two or more sheets of different colored veneers. Then the pieces were assembled in alternating colors to develop decorative contrasts. This method became popular during the reign of King Louis XIV. Shell, bone, wood and metal were sometimes used in the design. Materials could also be positioned both above and below the panel surface. Unfortunately, this form of furniture (also used for walls and floors) decoration deteriorates easily, and as a result, parts often become unglued from the surface.

While all of these intarsia methods are still in use today, only the first three—*tarsia certosima, tarsia geometrica* and *tarsia a toppo*—are done with any frequency except, of course, for restorations. For our purposes, intarsia is practically the same as marquetry. The main difference being that the former is traditional in practice while the latter is more contemporary.

If you would like to get in-depth information about both intarsia and marquetry, contact the Marquetry Society of America, P.O. Box 224, Lindenhurst, NY 11757. This is a complex subject, steeped in history, so we cannot cover more than the basics in this section.

One very good alterntive to creating intarsia designs is to purchase ready-made patterns from a wood or craft supply store. There are a number of mail-order companies that offer a good selection of intarsia designs. These can then be inlaid into veneer for decorating panels, furniture, boxes and other surfaces. Currently available are square, rectangular, round and oval designs.

Trace the pattern directly on the protective covering that comes on sheet plastic. This will minimize chipping and help the blade run cooler.

In our example we will use a round ready-made design and inlay it into a larger sheet of veneer. It is important that the thickness of both pieces be the same.

Begin by positioning the design on the larger sheet of veneer. You must decide how best to position for grain variations—two obvious choices are parallel and perpendicular. Once you are satisfied with the layout, trace around the edge of the inlay with a sharp pencil. This will be the cut line on the scroll saw.

Next, drill a suitable size pilot hole in the area to be cut out. Adjust the table on your scroll saw to make a 90° cut. Then, make the cut in a clockwise direction, keeping the blade just inside the cut line. After cutting, insert the pattern. It should fit snugly, with no visible spacing around the edges. If the pattern is too snug, lightly sand the edges for a good fit.

Now the design and larger veneer must be glued to a solid base board. For this you can use a light coating of woodworking glue and clamp the pieces until the glue hardens. As an alternative you can use contact cement.

GLOSSARY

Abrasive—any of the coated papers, fabrics or other materials, including pumice, rottenstone and steel wool, used for smoothing wood or between-coat smoothing of finishes.

Air-dried lumber—lumber that has been piled in yards or sheds for any length of time to reduce the natural moisture content of the wood. In the United States the minimum moisture content of thoroughly air-dried lumber is 12 to 15 percent.

Bar clamp—a clamping device with a long bar used to clamp the edges of wood when gluing panels or corners of boxes during assembly.

Bevel—to cut at an inclined or sloping edge rather than at a 90° angle.

Bits—boring tools of varying diameters used with an electric drill or a brace.

Bleeding—tendency of some bare woods to release color into a finish applied over them. Controllable through the use of sealers.

Boiled linseed oil—linseed oil in which enough lead, manganese or cobalt salts have been incorporated to make the oil harden more rapidly when spread in a thin coating.

Butt joint—a joint made by fastening wood end-to-end or edge-to-edge without overlap.

C-clamp—a steel-framed clamp, shaped like the letter C, for clamping small objects.

Chamfer—a beveled edge.

Checking—fissures that appear with age or drying in wood and finish coatings.

Close-grain wood—wood that does not reveal open pores when dry. Examples include maple, cherry and birch.

Column—a vertical freestanding support member.

Compound miter—a miter joint that incorporates a bevel.

Contact cement—a solvent-based cement that is applied to both surfaces to be joined and allowed to dry. Adhesion is immediate upon contact of the two surfaces.

Crocus cloth—an extremely fine abrasive used at the final stages of rubbing a finish, usually with a rubbing oil.

Dado—a groove cut in the edge, end or face of a board.

Dovetail joint—a traditional method of joining two pieces of wood in furniture construction. Distinguished by a fan-shaped tenon that forms a tight, interlocking joint when fitted into a corresponding mortise.

Enamel—name given to color finishes with a high varnish content, similar to varnish in handling and protection.

Figured veneer—veneer cut from a portion of the tree where the grain pattern is distorted.

Filler—a heavily pigmented preparation used for filling and leveling off the pores in open-pored woods.

Flat finish—a paint or other finish that contains a high proportion of pigment and dries to a flat or lusterless finish.

Flat grain—flat-grained lumber has been sawed parallel to the pith of the log and approximately tangent to the growth rings, i.e., the rings form an angle of less than 45° with the surface of the piece.

Glossy finish—a paint or enamel that contains a relatively low proportion of pigment and dries to a sheen or luster.

Grain—the direction, size, arrangement, appearance or quality of the fibers in wood.

Grain edge (vertical)—edge-grain lumber has been sawed parallel to the pith of the log and approximately at right angles to the growth rings; i.e., the rings form an angle of 45° or more with the surface of the piece.

Hardwood—wood from deciduous trees.

Heartwood—the wood extending from the pith to the sapwood, the cells of which no longer participate in the life process of the tree.

Inlay—a piece of wood or other material set into a background piece of wood.

Intarsia—an Italian term for marquetry.

Kerf—a cut made by a saw.

Kiln-dried lumber—lumber that has been kiln dried, often to a moisture content of 6 to 12 percent. Common varieties of softwood lumber, such as framing lumber, are dried to a somewhat higher moisture content.

Knot—in lumber, the portion of a branch or limb of a tree that appears on the edge or face of the piece.

Laminating—the bonding together of multiple layers of wood; used to achieve greater strength and thickness as well as for decorative purposes.

Latex—generic term used to cover a variety of finishes and paints that use water as a thinner.

Lumber—lumber is the product of the sawmill and planing mill not further manufactured other than by sawing, resawing, and passing lengthwise through a standard planing machine, crosscutting to length and matching.

Marquetry—a form of inlay. The term usually refers to elaborate patterns of inlay using many different colored woods in veneer form.

Mineral spirits—paint thinners and brush cleaners made as derivatives of oil.

Natural finish—a transparent finish that does not seriously alter the original color or grain of the natural wood. Natural finishes are usually provided by sealers, oils, varnishes, water-repellent preservatives and other similar materials.

Oil stain—stains formed by mixing oil-soluble dyes in an oil or oleoresinous base. The term is sometimes applied to pigmented wiping stains, which may also contain pigments in suspension.

Overlay—commonly a veneer used for decoration when applied to a surface.

Paste filler—common wood filler, in paste form, which must be reduced before application.

Plywood—a piece of wood made of three or more layers of veneer joined with glue, and usually laid with the grain of adjoining plies at right angles. Almost always an odd number of plies are used to provide balanced construction.

Polyurethane—chemical term applied to oil-modified urethane varnishes that do not require hardeners or moisture curing but dry through evaporation.

Primer—the first coat in a paint job that consists of two or more coats; also the paint used for such a first coat.

Raw linseed oil—the crude product processed from flaxseed and usually without much subsequent treatment.

Sapwood—the outer zone of wood, next to the bark. In the living tree, it contains some living cells (the heartwood contains none), as well as dead and dying cells. In most species, it is lighter colored than the heartwood. In all species, it is lacking in decay resistance.

Sealer—a finishing material, either clear or pigmented, that is usually applied directly over uncoated wood for the purpose of sealing the surface.

Seasoning—to remove moisture from green wood in order to improve its serviceability.

Semigloss finish—a paint, enamel or varnish made with a slight insufficiency of nonvolatile vehicle so that its coating, when dry, has some luster but is not very glossy.

Set—for adhesives, to harden.

Softwood—woods of the coniferous group.

Spar varnish—name given to varnishes intended for outdoor use, most often phenolic-resin varnishes. The term has little meaning, except that materials labeled spar are usually of good quality.

Spray—to apply a finish by means of spray equipment or aerosol spray cans.

Stain—any material used to change the natural color of wood.

Toenail—to drive a nail at a slant to the initial surface in order to permit it to penetrate into a second member.

Topcoat—any finishing material used over another. In practical terms, the final coat of a finish.

Veneer—a thin layer of wood or other material.

Varnish—a thickened preparation of drying oil, or drying oil and resin, suitable for spreading on surfaces to form continuous, transparent coatings, or for mixing with pigments to make enamels.

Water stain—an aniline dye stain made by dissolving soluble dyes in water. Water stains are considered by many to be the best colors and the most durable.

Wood chisel—a flat metal tool with a sharpened edge for chipping, carving or shaving wood.

Wood filler—the same as paste filler. A material used to fill the open pores—grain—of the wood so that subsequent finishes are entirely level.

INDEX

More Great Books for Your Woodshop!

Build Your Own Router Tables—Increase your router's accuracy, versatility and usefulness with a winning table design. Detailed plans and instructions for 3 types of tables plus a variety of specialty jigs and fixtures will help you create the right table for your shop. *#70367/$21.99/160 pages/300 illus./paperback*

The Encyclopedia of Joint Making—Create the best joints for every project! This comprehensive resource shows you how to prepare lumber, prevent layout errors, select the right joint, choose the best fastener and more. *#70356/$22.99/144 pages/300+ color illus.*

The Woodworker's Guide to Furniture Design—Discover what it takes to design visually pleasing and comfortably functional furniture. Garth Graves shows you how to blend aesthetics and function with construction methods and material characteristics to develop designs that really work! *#70355/$27.99/208 pages/110 illus.*

Build Your Own Entertainment Centers—Now you can customize the construction and design of an entertainment center to fit your skill level, tools, style and budget. With this heavily illustrated guidebook, you'll explore the whole process—from selecting the wood to hardware and finishing. *#70354/$22.99/128 pages/paperback*

Good Wood Finishes—Take the mystery out of one of woodworking's most feared tasks! With detailed instructions and illustrations you'll learn about applying the perfect finish, preparing materials, repairing aged finishes, graining wood and much more. *#70343/$19.99/128 pages/325+ color illus.*

Measure Twice, Cut Once, Revised Edition—Miscalculation will be a thing of the past when you learn these effective techniques for checking and adjusting measuring tools, laying out complex measurements, fixing mistakes, making templates and much more! *#70330/$22.99/144 pages/144 color illus.*

How To Sharpen Every Blade in Your Woodshop—You know that tools perform best when razor sharp—yet you avoid the dreaded chore. This ingenious guide brings you plans for jigs and devices that make sharpening any blade short and simple! Includes jigs for sharpening boring tools, router bits and more! *#70250/$17.99/144 pages/157 b&w illus./paperback*

100 Keys to Woodshop Safety—Make your shop safer than ever with this manual designed to help you avoid potential pitfalls. Tips and illustrations demonstrate the basics of safe shopwork—from using electricity safely and avoiding trouble with hand and power tools to ridding your shop of dangerous debris and handling finishing materials. *#70333/$17.99/64 pages/125 color illus./paperback*

Making Elegant Gifts From Wood—Develop your woodworking skills and make over 30 gift-quality projects at the same time! You'll find everything you're looking to create in your gifts—variety, timeless styles, pleasing proportions and imaginative designs that call for the best woods. Plus, technique sidebars and hardware installation tips make your job even easier. *#70331/$24.99/128 pages/30 color, 120 b&w illus.*

Getting the Very Best From Your Router—Get to know your router inside and out as you discover new jigs and fixtures to amplify its capabilities, as well as techniques to make it the most precise cutting tool in your shop. Plus, tips for comparing different routers and bits will help you buy smart for a solid long-term investment. *#70328/$22.99/144 pages/225+ b&w illus.*

Good Wood Handbook, 2nd Edition—Now you can select and use the right wood for the job—before you buy. You'll discover valuable information on a wide selection of commercial softwoods and hardwoods—from common uses, color and grain to how the wood glues and takes finish. *#70329/$19.99/128 pages/250 color illus.*

100 Keys to Preventing & Fixing Woodworking Mistakes—Stop those mistakes before they happen—and fix those that have already occurred. Numbered tips and color illustrations show you how to work around flaws in wood; fix mistakes made with the saw, plane, router and lathe; repair badly made joints, veneering mishaps and finishing blunders; assemble projects successfully; and more! *#70332/$17.99/64 pages/125 color illus.*

Creating Your Own Woodshop—Discover dozens of economical ways to fill unused space with the woodshop of your dreams. Self shows you how to convert space, lay out the ideal woodshop, or improve your existing shop. *#70229/$18.99/128 pages/162 b&w photos/illus./paperback*

Tables You Can Customize—Learn how to build four types of basic tables—from a Shaker coffee table to a Stickley library table—then discover how to apply a wide range of variations to customize the pieces to fit your personal needs. *#70299/$19.99/128 pages/150 b&w illus./paperback*

The Woodworker's Sourcebook, 2nd Edition—Shop for woodworking supplies from home! Self has compiled listings for everything from books and videos to plans and associations. Each listing has an address and telephone number and is rated in terms of quality and price. *#70281/$19.99/160 pages/50 illus.*

Basic Woodturning Techniques—Detailed explanations of fundamental techniques like faceplate and spindle turning will have you turning beautiful pieces in no time. *#70211/$14.95/112 pages/119 b&w illus./paperback*

The Stanley Book of Woodworking Tools, Techniques and Projects—Become a better woodworker by mastering the fundamentals of choosing the right wood, cutting tight-fitting joints, properly using a marking gauge and much more. *#70264/$19.95/160 pages/400 color illus./paperback*

Good Wood Routers—Get the most from your router with this comprehensive guide to hand-held power routers and table routing. You'll discover a world of information about types of routers, their uses, maintenance, setup, precision table routing and much, much more. *#70319/$19.99/128 pages/550 color illus.*

Tune Up Your Tools—Bring your tools back to perfect working order and experience safe, accurate cutting, drilling and sanding. With this handy reference you'll discover how to tune up popular woodworking machines, instructions for aligning your tools, troubleshooting charts and many other tips. *#70308/$22.99/144 pages/150 b&w illus./paperback*